LACES

A Boys of Hawthorne Asylum Novel (#1)

TEMPI LARK

-M

Tempe xo

LACES

BOYS OF HAWTHORNE ASYLUM

Edited by: Sara Miller, Pretty Little Book Promotions

Cover Designer: Mayhem Cover Creations

www.tempilark.com

TEMPI LARK

Mailing List

To keep up to date with Tempi's writing and more, sign up for her newsletter.

Click the link below to sign up.
https://bit.ly/3iTJsba

Author's Note

I contracted Covid-19 TWICE while writing Laces, which lead to sickness and physical weakness (and other things, but we won't go into that lol). I would like to thank my editor, PR team, Street Team, and readers for being patient with me during my recovery.

Disclaimer

Laces was originally intended to be a standalone, but was later changed to a series to lessen my stress during the illness. Laces contains strong language/cursing, sexual and physical abuse, and other triggering scenes that might not be suitable for everybody. There are Reverse Harem themes at play throughout the series. This book is an angsty slow burn that builds toward intimate scenes as the series progresses, and is not intended for readers under 17. *Laces is book one in the Boys of Hawthorne Asylum series*

Playlist

Praying - Kesha
Sweet but Psycho – Ava Max
Lights – Elle Goulding
Seein' Red - Unwritten Law
Broken – LovelyTheBand
My Kind of Love – Leon Else
Always Hate Me – James Blunt
Wakey Wakey – NCT 127
Whatever It Takes – Imagine Dragons
Confessions of a Broken Heart – Lindsay Lohan
If You Could See Me Now – The Script
Like a Stone – Audioslave
Secret Love Song – Little Mix, feat. Jason Derulo
Dusk Till Dawn – ZAYN, feat. Sia
Make It Right – BTS, feat. Lauv
Desert Rose – Sting
I'm Alive – Celine Dion
Sound of Your Heart – Shawn Hook
Independent Love Song – Scarlett
Husavik – Will Ferrell, My Marianne

Find the playlist that inspired Laces on Spotify!

Dedication

For anyone who has ever been abandoned.
This one's for you.

"Love is my religion—I could die for it."

-John Keats-

Prologue

DA's daughter declared legally insane; will join the Legendary Three at Hawthorne Asylum.

By Samantha Malley, The Weekly Enquirer.

GAMBRIELLE EVANS, the stepdaughter of Charlotte District Attorney, Joseph Evans, was declared by a judge to be mentally unstable Thursday morning. The nineteen-year-old was taken into custody shortly after ten a.m. and hauled away in a police cruiser while a crowd of fifty or so looked on from the courthouse. This news comes exactly one day after a grand jury dismissed murder charges against the district attorney, in the death of his stepdaughter, Elizabeth Evans, who was found in bed, unresponsive, at the family's Charlotte estate six months earlier.

"Regardless of the fact if Gambrielle was telling the truth about what she saw that night, or if it was something her mind conjured up to deal with the traumatic loss, we might never know what really happened. What we do know is the statement she provided to the prosecution does not match up with the evidence." Sheriff Thompson said at a news briefing. When asked by a reporter to elaborate upon the last part of his statement, Sheriff Thompson didn't hold back, "The evidence doesn't lie. People do."

Ms. Evans initially claimed that she was hiding in her sister's closet during the murder, but later retracted her statement when her mother told prosecutors that they were together that day visiting a close friend. Sources say the close friend even validated the claim, which didn't aid the prosecution when the time came to get an indictment.

Joseph Evans' attorney, Thomas Newman, issued this statement today:

Attorney Joseph Evans is an upstanding, valuable member of our community here in Charlotte. He has gone above and beyond during his twenty years of public service, and the accusations that were brought against him in no way reflect who he is, or the work he has performed for the community. He is eager to get back to work and return to some normalcy. He would like to thank everyone for their support during this trying time and asks that you respect his family's privacy as they try and move forward in the next stages of healing.

Though it hasn't been confirmed by Charlotte officials, sources closely connected with the case say Ms. Evans will be admitted to Hawthorne Asylum in the coming days. The mental hospital is well known for housing notorious high-profile patients, such as the Legendary Three, and has often been criticized for its unorthodox treatment methods.

COMMENTS (2,513)

MattAtYou
Damn. O_O Judge Wexler threw the book at her. Ruthless.

Pumpkin_bliss
Nothing to see here. Just another rich girl screaming for attention.

XJordanSkiesX
Housed with The Legendary Three? You act like that's a *real* punishment. US WOMEN KNOW BETTER! ROTFLMAO.

Marie7210
I volunteer to be locked up with Laces!

Gemma_Light12
Laces is so fuckin hot!

Marie7210
Yes he is! I would sleep with all three. IDGAF.

DarwinB89
Strange what women find attractive these days…

KellyDCloveX
Do they provide condoms in the nuthouse? Asking for a friend…

Marie7210
THIS.

ONE

Gambrielle

I ALWAYS THOUGHT the first time I stripped would be for a man. Nothing big. A little decoration here and there, a pair of sexy underwear, and Usher's sweet voice to drive it home.

"Jeans. Shirt. Flats. Everything has to go." Nurse Kline said, sounding unmoved as she peeked over her tablet. Shell-shocked, I was still standing in the same corner of the small room—shoulders slumped, bug-eyed, mouth hinged open. *Has it really come to this?* "Did you hear me, Evans?"

Her mouth, I could see it moving—the angry expression spreading across her pores, but I still couldn't make sense of it all.

She wants you to strip.

Yes.

Take everything off.

What for?

On any other day, I would've been able to connect the dots.

When I didn't immediately obey her command, Nurse

Kline tucked the tablet under her arm and cocked her head to the side. Examining me from head-to-toe, she said, "You are Gambrielle Evans, correct?"

I didn't answer.

The tablet was back in her hand so fast, and she was scrolling down to the bottom, "You know what, this would go a lot smoother if you would at least acknowledge my questions." She took a quick glance at me. "You are Gambrielle Evans correct? You were ordered here by Judge Wexler until the doctors on staff deem you are no longer a threat to society."

All I could do was nod. *Yep.*

Her eyes were back on her tablet as she mouthed, *ohhh-kay.* Pointing at an empty plastic tote near the door, she said, "Put your clothes and shoes in there."

Excuse me???

My stepfather, Joe, was probably cracking jokes at that very moment, proudly reminiscing about my takedown with all of his lawyer buddies. The image of him toasting and taking a swig of his whiskey with the rich bastards that had aided in my inevitable downfall was almost too much to fathom——"Evans?"

——you don't belong here.

"EVANS?"

Pursing my lips, I tore my eyes away from the tablet and looked straight into Nurse Kline's watchful gaze. I knew deep down that my current dilemma wasn't her fault, but that didn't stop the thoughts running through my head. She was admitting me to *Hell* and therefore was a part of the problem. "He did it." I finally said with conviction. Whether or not she knew what I was referring to, I didn't know or care. I needed to speak my peace on the matter.

Ignoring me, she jerked her chin toward the tote again. "Put all of your stuff in there."

With a heavy sigh, I bent over and started to remove one of my flats, but stilled when I saw Nurse Kline slapping on a pair of white latex gloves. *Oh no...* my brows drew in. I could hear my heart pounding through my ears, feel my hands trembling in midair. Only when she proceeded to grab the KY jelly did I finally speak up. "Wait, wait-wait—what are you doing? Wh-h-hat do you need that for?" I already knew, but was holding on to hope that maybe I would be the exception.

"It's protocol. No one enters Hawthorne Asylum without passing inspection." Like toothpaste, she poured a generous amount of the clear liquid on two bony fingers and smirked at me. "It'll be quick."

I didn't think.

I didn't speak.

I just acted.

One second I was standing in front of Nurse Kline contemplating the integrity of my nether region—and the next I was a football star, faking to the left and right, snaking around her small frame and darting for the wooden door. "Calm down, Evans! Relax!"

But it was too late. I'd already flung the door open and was racing down the sterile, white hallway, arms pumping back and forth, my years of running track being put to the ultimate test.

The intercom sounded right as I raced past what appeared to be the nurse's station. "Code red, Floor B." Three orderlies scrambled to get out of their leather chairs as their leader shouted off rapid-fire instructions in his radio, "Get a tranq!"

Everything was glaringly white: the floor, walls, ceiling, desks... The smell of ammonia slammed into my lungs, briefly catching me off guard, but I forged ahead like a wild animal, zig-zagging through the long hallway.

"Code red, Floor B."

"She is not sticking those sausages in my butt!" I roared at the ceiling, hoping if there was a camera whoever was behind it would see. "She. Will. Not. Violate. Meeee!" It was a bit melodramatic, I'll admit, but my ass was on the line. *Literally*.

Everything played out in slow motion. I could see myself running—see the patients shooting me curious glances, a mixture of interest and fear entering their eyes as they realized what direction I was heading toward: the cracked door at the end of the hall. I'd pegged it as my safe place the second I saw all three orderlies hot on my tail.

"Shit, she's going to Laces!" I heard one of the orderlies shout right as my black flats slid across the marble floor. Thrusting my arm forward, I grabbed the doorknob, stumbling on shaky knees as I attempted to regain my balance —"Hey no! You don't want to do that! Listen to me—"

—and get two fingers shoved up my ass? Hard pass. The choice was a no-brainer for me. Once I caught my bearings, I lunged into the room and slammed the door behind me, my back sliding down the cold metal as my knees slowly collapsed. My hands tented over my nose. "Shhh… breathe…you're mommy's little bumblebee…you're a bumblebee, yes you are. You're a bumblebee to the stars. You're a bumblebee, yes you are. You're mommy's little bumblebee." I hummed the song at least three or four times while imagining the secret closet in my old basement. *Safe. Secluded.* Whenever my nerves got the best of me, that small room hidden behind a wine cellar became my refuge from any and all chaos. It had seen me through some dark days.

You shouldn't be here.

No.

I repeated the same chorus a couple more times, until

my heart found a steady rhythm, and then opened my eyes. Orderlies were pounding on the door, the vibrations of their fists slamming into my back as Nurse Kline begged for me to come out—but I barely heard anything because of *him*. He was lying back on his twin bed in the furthest corner, his attentive blue eyes peeking over the sketchpad in his hand. I'd seen a lot of men in my lifetime, a lot of attractive men…the guy sitting on that bed was not a man. *No*. The very word seemed offensive for someone of his caliber. He looked like a model that had just stepped off of the runway in Paris—long, silky black strands falling into his eyes, thick lips, and a taut, lean body. His arms were well defined, each muscle curving smoothly into the next… he was a vision, like one of the men on my grandma's favorite romance novels.

And I'd like to say that I played it cool, that I rose to my feet and put my best southern manners forward and extended my hand and introduced myself as the newest patient of Asheville's most notorious asylum for troubled youth.

But my eyes started to wander—and the sketches hung around the room suddenly came into view. *Dead women… dead women everywhere*. My throat constricted. *Oh God*…my eyes flew every which way, taking in the scene before me, all of the Hannibal-Lecter-like sketches proudly displayed around the small confined space.

Oops…

I had picked the wrong room.

Clearly…

Suddenly I felt dizzy and hot.

Out of the corner of my eye I spotted Hannibal Sketcher as he rose from his bed. The shadow of his six-foot frame towered over me as I scrambled to find the doorknob behind me. *No, no, no…*The word "help" was on the tip of my tongue, but it never made it out. My heart was in a new state of panic, my breathing ragged…my eyes rolled back and my body suddenly turned limp. The last thing I saw before the darkness overtook me was the floor rushing up to greet me.

TWO

Laces

_____

SHE LOOKED like a scared kitten that had just escaped a potential downpour. Her wide, brown eyes were blazing with fear, her arms and legs shaking as she tried to process everything. I'd seen that kind of fear before, the—my life is over, what's the point in trying—fear that seemed to fill the air when no bright light could be found at the end of the tunnel. For four years I'd watched it suck the life out of my mother, watched her die right before my eyes, and though I knew it was useless, I'd fought tooth and nail to bring just an ounce of her light back.

That was what drew me to _her_ in the first place.

The need to protect her, to guide her through this hell, seemed to overpower the walls that I'd built around myself to keep my human instincts at bay. The urge to reach out and touch her, to ask—no, demand—what was wrong, paralyzed me. In the two years leading up to her arrival, I'd made peace with my situation; It wasn't the life I'd pictured for myself, but was definitely better than the life I had grown up in and been forced to accept.

The tip of my pencil had punctured my sketchpad,

creating a small hole in the arm of my latest sketch, resembling a mole, but I didn't give a damn. Not today, anyway. Her eyes roamed over my body, stopping at the pencil pressed deep against my forefinger. I wondered if she would start singing again—*or breakout in prayer*—which was customary for newbies. Both seemed plausible. But instead her eyes slowly drifted to the wall, to a land of death and despair, and what fear she had entered my domain with escalated to catastrophic proportions.

Fuck.

Lifting my palms, I carefully rose from the bed, my sketchpad and pencil clattering to the floor with a deafening echo. My mouth opened, the word "easy" was poised on the tip of my tongue, but before it could pass through my lips her eyes rolled back and her lifeless body fell to the floor.

"Are you fuckin' kidding me?" I muttered under my breath. Normally women were throwing themselves at me —proposing fuckin' marriage—but not this one. This *stray* had cowered away and completely shut down.

"Where is a camera when you need one?" My buddy, Reyes, chuckled from behind. I glanced over my shoulder to see him curled up in a dark corner, an apple in his hand. Taking a bite, he gestured with his chin toward the scene displayed before him. "Smooth. Very smooth."

I rolled my eyes. "Fuck off."

"She saw you coming from a mile away. '*No I don't want your autograph, get me the hell outta here.*'" Reyes snickered. "She's a smart girl. I like her."

I shot him an arrogant grin. "Maybe she fainted because of me? Did you ever think of that?" I challenged, knowing damn well that was not the case. My ego had taken a major hit and I was grabbing at every straw at the bar. "She's probably never seen this much man. Didn't know what to do with all this masculinity."

Reyes' eyes flew over my shoulder, to where Stray's lifeless body laid. He smirked. "Oh, she knew exactly what to do, trust me." *Fuckwad*. He gestured toward her body, which was splayed out like a chalk outline at a crime scene. "You better take advantage of your muse before Kline sends her lackeys in, tranq guns blazing."

"How can you think about art at a time like this?"

"How can you not?" And when I didn't jump to get my sketchpad, he shook his head in dismay, a knowing grin spread across his lips. She had fallen to the floor on her side—both arms clutching her chest, one leg shot out—like someone who had tried to run. Had it been anyone else I would've dropped to my knees and started sketching away, letting the strokes take me to a place that made sense. But I couldn't do that with her. I didn't want to.

For the first time in a while, I wanted to feel something. Anything. I wanted to embed this memory into my brain for a rainy day, just in case I got a wild hair in my ass in the future and wanted to feel it again. As I enclosed the space between us, the voices in my head started their provoking pleas, demanding I shut it off, but I couldn't. I was too far gone. Kneeling down beside her, I made a mental note to retain this in my memory; her jeans, black flats, and checkered button up blouse. Even the stray hair that had gotten trapped in the corner of her pouty lips—committed to memory. With twitchy fingers I reached forward to brush away the stray strand, but caught myself when Reyes warned from behind, "you'll lose points."

I looked around the empty room. "Who is going to tell? The women on my walls? They're already dead." Everyone had that one friend, the one who couldn't live just to live, who couldn't take risks without evaluating all of the small details. That was Reyes. *But Laces, what if you fuck her and she ends up pregnant and births your firstborn in the nuthouse*—he'd said that very phrase on a constant loop when I first started inviting women to my room for a little humpty-humpty. He was always worried about the consequences and couldn't see the worthy opportunities when they presented themselves.

Like now.

I had an opportunity to get up close and personal with a newbie from the outside, and all Reyes was worried about was a few damn points.

A pirate grin crept across my lips.

We weren't allowed to touch other patients at the asylum. It was near the top of the rules list, right below trying to butcher your wrist with a plastic fork, and calling your buddy on the outside to come up with an escape plan to get your ass out. I'd never given a damn about the rules or trying to obey them, so starting to give a fuck now seemed pointless.

I looked back at Reyes. His curious eyes were trained on me with a hint of confusion I didn't quite understand. Moments ago he had been urging me to sketch, but now was silent. "You're not going to try and stop me?" I asked. Out of the three of us—Reyes, me, and Thorne—Reyes was the closest one to sane, according to our charts. He was the paranoid one. The serious one. The one always trying to keep us out of trouble. He was the conscience we never had, and during times like this I depended on him to pull me back to my humanity. But he seemed in no hurry to do that.

Taking another bite of his apple, he chewed, watching in silence as I gave into my urges and stroked a piece of her soft, curly brown hair. It was stupid, needing Reyes' supervision for what most thought was a basic task, but it was a necessity. The one thing I'd never learned in life was how to stop—how to just throw in the towel and give up, in order to move on. My brain didn't know how to process *the end*. It couldn't accept defeat. All it knew was how to keep fighting, like I had with my mother. It was a trait I applied in all aspects of my life, and this moment was no different. That was part of the reason I was at Hawthorne to begin with, obsessing over stupid shit. And at the moment I was obsessing over the texture of the curly strand in between my fingers.

"Let go." I heard Reyes whisper. "Don't think about what you want, think about what she wants. She is unconscious, Laces."

"It'll be okay. I can handle it." That was a lie, but it was a worthy one, nonetheless. At least to me. I wanted to let her go, really I did. I knew letting her go was the right thing, the humane thing. Women like her and men like me didn't belong together. I was fearless, careless, and above all else, reckless. And yet every time I tried to release a curl, to release the sweet intoxicating scent that eluded her, something would pull me back. The curly strand, the way it was tightly wound around my fingers, forced other urges to come to light.

My eyes fell to her hands clutching her chest, her pale fingers shielding her breasts as if they knew I was coming. Reyes was right: *smart girl*.

"I want to see her palms." I said, looking back at Reyes. His eyes had widened to the point I swore they would pop out at any moment. "Her hair is nothing but a tease, alright? If I'm going to do this, I want to fully commit." Again, *obsessive issues*.

"Spoken like a true psychopath." Reyes mused.

I shot him a go-to-hell-look. My ass was never getting out of Hawthorne anyway, so I might as well make it worth my while. It was a terrible mindset to have, one that Dr. Young had spent the last three months hounding me about in therapy, but right then I didn't give a shit. Like a caveman that had just discovered his first pussy, I spread her arms open and took it all in—her milky, white skin and the bluish veins leading up her forearms. Somewhere along the way to my room she'd cut her wrist and a pool of blood had begun to form in the crook of her elbow. It was then while trying to search for the source of the bleeding that I noticed the branded JE initials on her wrist. "How did you brand yourself?" I whispered to her. I'd seen many cuts and burns pass through the asylum, but never a brand. Branding was for cattle, a permanent way to show what was yours. Trailing my finger over the welt, my heart picked up a little speed at the thought of this petite woman sitting in her room, sock shoved in her mouth, the smell of flesh burning…

Like a loyal hobbit, Reyes piped in, "What are you waiting for?"

"She branded herself." I murmured.

Reyes sat his apple on the floor and jumped to his feet. Making it to me in two quick strides, he said, "that's her problem. Let her go."

Two swift knocks came at my door, followed by Nurse Kline's voice, "Gambrielle? Come on out, honey."

Gambrielle?

Reyes cursed.

Ignoring Nurse Kline, I hastily grabbed Gambrielle's right wrist and turned it over, inspecting it as I had done with her left. There were no markings, which was weird. One arm was beautiful, the other tormented. "Why would she brand herself with JE—it doesn't make sense." I shook my head. "Cutters are wild. They don't give a fuck."

"Stop obsessing!" Reyes whispered with a hiss. He

grabbed a handful of the back of my hoodie and yanked me to a standing position. My brain was still a hazy shit-storm of thoughts from the emotions running through my mind—the stray, my mother, Nurse Kline, the branding. Placing both hands on my shoulders, Reyes squeezed, hard.

"Listen to me. Nurse Kline is outside YOUR door."

I blinked twice. "Okay." *But the branding…*

Reyes tapped the side of my head. "You have a library of *Playboy Magazine's* laying around your room."

My heart stopped dead in its tracks and my eyes widened. "Oh shit."

"Oh shit is right, my friend."

My fear of solitary outweighed my need to hold onto to Gambrielle—yes—but I refused to leave empty-handed. As Reyes started shoving the magazines underneath my bed, I snaked a pair of scissors I had hidden inside of my mattress and made quick work of parting Gambrielle's hair.

"What are you doing?" Reyes whispered with a hiss. Like a conveyor belt, he slung another magazine under the bed. "Solitary is waiting outside your door! We don't have time for this shit! Fuckin' crazy ass!" *Yes, yes I was.*

"I've got it under control!" I shot back.

"Bullshit! Let her go!"

"I will! As soon as I cut this." I swore. "You have to look at this from my point of view: what if she doesn't talk to me, hmm? What will I do then?" Scoffing at my friend, I turned to Gambrielle and, like a crazed barber, used my fingers to pull the curly lock to an even angle. "This will tide me over until I can figure out my next move."

Reyes' hands flew to his head. "Easy, Sweeney Todd. Are you even listening to yourself right now?"

Scissors ready, I cut a thick curly strand from her hair and quickly shoved it into my pocket.

Another knock came at the door, along with a final ultimatum. "Gambrielle? If you don't come out, we're gonna have to send security in."

I didn't feel the slightest twinge of remorse for cutting Gambrielle's hair. In fact, all I could do was smile. Fuckin' smile. Even after the orderlies broke through the door like the secret service and pinned my face to the floor, my lips kissing the scuffed surface's ass, all I could do was smile.

THREE

Gambrielle

"I look like a doll!"

"But a beautiful doll." My mother pointed out, reaching for the big red bow on top of my white dresser. She had found it at a thrift shop at the beginning of the summer and was saving it for just this special occasion. Staring at my four-foot reflection, I watched as my mother pulled a few auburn strands away from my porcelain face and smiled at her handiwork. "First impressions are important, Gambrielle. It's your first day at a new school, you need to look nice."

I crossed my arms and huffed. "I want to wear my glitter shirt!"

My mother had fixed herself up that morning. I didn't know where she got it, but the red dress she was wearing looked like it cost a million dollars. Her once fuzzy, brown hair was now curly and shiny; her face painted up like one of those ladies we always saw going into the expensive purse stores. We could never afford to buy anything from there, but that never stopped us from standing outside the window and pointing at the different purses we would buy when we won the lottery. Or in my mother's case, won a rich man.

Even as a naïve ten-year-old, I still noticed her desire for the finer things in life. The way she picked up my new backpack from my ratty old twin bed, her fingers running across the LV logo imprinted in the white leather like it was a rare jewel.

And I supposed to her it was. "I already told you: you can't wear the glitter shirt. This school is different. They have a uniform policy." She studied me through her long lashes. "That's why you look like a doll."

The navy blue pleated skirt was itchy and hung just above my knees. My mother said it complimented the navy blue blazer and white polo that I was also forced to wear, but I didn't see it. All I saw was one of my dress-up dolls preparing to play a part.

"Alright, let's put this on and," my mother's eyes lit up as she hooked my backpack straps through my arms, "it's perfect. You look perfect."

"I don't feel perfect." I mumbled to my reflection.

My mother dusted the lint off of my shoulders, "Well, you need to start. There are going to be a lot of positive changes around here over the next few weeks and I need your support, okay?" I nodded. She knelt down to eye level and pushed a runaway auburn curl behind my ear, "no more secondhand clothes, understand? No more cold baths, or beans for dinner." Her smile was big, but sad as she tapped my tiny nose.

"You're going to have the life I never had."

My lips quirked up.

"Now," My mother rose to her feet and clapped her hands twice, the fresh white paint at the tip of her nails shining like a new diamond, "let's get the Princess to her new castle, shall we?"

"Yes!" Her excitement was contagious.

I grabbed her hand, and we made our way through our tiny one-bedroom apartment. "I also have another surprise for you." My mother said as she unlocked the front door, "Mommy has a new friend who has been kind enough to give us a ride today. I need you to behave okay?" I nodded.

We stepped out onto the wooden porch and my eyes immediately flew to the shiny red SUV parked a few feet away. Inside an older man, maybe in his mid-forties, with salt and pepper hair and a tight smile, waved at me. There was no happiness in his dark eyes, no kindness in the way he introduced himself.

The man's name was Joe, and as I soon learned, he would give us everything our hearts desired.

He also killed our hearts in the process.

AMMONIA, fresh linen, and the sound of a wrapper tearing open—pulled me out of whatever comatose state I'd been in. Disoriented, I could still hear *their* feet padding throughout the room, instruments dropping against a metal tray... *Where am I?* And the even more pressing question, what were they doing to me?

Someone let out a low curse, and an instrument clattered onto a tray. *Oh God. What did Hannibal Sketcher do to me?* I swallowed slowly, hoping no one saw—out of sight, out of mind, I kept repeating that phrase over and over in a bid to remain calm.

All I could remember was seeing *his* face coming closer, the demonic sketches of women—some clothed, some not —bloody appendages galore, limbs barely hanging on. Just thinking about it was enough to send me into a full-blown panic attack. I was born and raised in a small country town where everyone knew everyone, and the gossip mill ran rampant. The talk of the town usually revolved around underage pregnancies, or the latest prostitute to take up the corner on Broad Street. That was the closest to screwed up as any of us ever saw. *Until I saw him, that is...* "Did you watch the case?" A feminine voice asked.

A deep voice piped in seconds later, "Are you kidding? Everyone in America watched that case." I felt a sharp tug at my elbow.

"You think she was telling the truth?"

"What do you think?" The deep somber voice asked.

He did it. No matter what anyone in this godforsaken world believed, he did it. *I know he did.* And I had made it my lifelong goal to prove it, so no one else had to endure what my family did.

There was a moment of silence, and then the woman murmured, "I think if she was telling the truth she wouldn't be in here."

"Exactly."

A few minutes later I heard a door shut, and a different set of footsteps enter. The sound of a lab coat brushing against the counter and a file opening forced me to crack open my eyes. The bright overhead light blinded me for a second and I squinted, catching a glimpse of an old man dragging a stool toward my bed. *No-no-no-no!* He wasted no time getting comfortable, propping his penny loafers on the bed railing. "I know you're awake, Gambrielle. The cameras caught you moving around while you were getting your stitches." he said matter-of-factly. "You had a bit of a nasty fall when you passed out, but no matter. In a week's time you'll be as good as new."

*So that's what they were doing...*not wanting to feel like a bigger idiot, I opened my eyes all the way and studied Dr...*what does his name tag say? Folton?* "Dr. Folton." He answered as if reading my thoughts. "You may call me Dr. Folton, Folton, or Doc. It doesn't matter to me. Whatever you are comfortable with." Glancing at the folder that was now splayed out on my bed he said, "You were court ordered to undergo a psychiatric evaluation. You failed, *obviously*...or else you wouldn't be in here."

"He did it." I blurted out, and Dr. Folton didn't acknowledge my claim as he continued to flip through page after page, checking for anything of vital importance.

"Hey, did you hear me?" I asked after ten seconds had passed. Normally I was a well behaved southern girl, my manners impeccable, but after everything that had transpired in the last six months, my patience had worn a bit thin. The way Dr. Folton ignored me, practically writing me off before I even had a chance to defend myself, *no.*

Like a vampire, my body rose from the bed and my eyes snapped to his direction. Slamming my hand over whatever paragraph held his interest and I shouted, "Stop reading those lies and listen to me! Joe wants to be rid of me, okay? I know the truth! He murdered my sister!" I jerked my hand back and gestured toward the messy papers, "All this is, is a cover-up to save his own ass!"

Dr. Folton offered a tight smile. "Is that right?" And it was the way he said it, like I was a lying toddler that sparked a fury deep within my bones. His bushy gray eyebrows lifted as he asked, "And who is Joe? Is he in here?"

"What?"

"Is Joe an imaginary friend?" he continued, whipping an ink pen out of the breast pocket of his white lab coat. All humor was gone—his gray eyes had turned serious. "Do you talk to him every day, or does he only come around when your anxiety hits its peak?"

I blinked. "Joe is my stepfather…"

"The man you accused of murdering your sister, correct?" Not daring to look up, he went on, "you know it's not nice to lie, Gambrielle?"

"I'm not lying."

"The state of North Carolina would beg to differ."

His words—so devoid of emotions—were like a knife to my chest. I wanted to cry, that seemed like a reasonable response that no one would've shamed me for, but I didn't. Because I got the feeling that was what Dr. Folton wanted, to see me weak and use it as a driving force to confirm what Judge Wexler already believed.

No.

I wasn't giving him the satisfaction.

Closing my file with a swish, Dr. Folton uncrossed his legs and rose to his feet. "In the forty-eight years I've been practicing medicine I've dealt with many of your kind, *girl*. You're selfish, entitled. You can try to convince me of your innocence, but I think we both know your words will fall on deaf ears around here." An arrogant smile tugged at the corner of his lips. "Here at Hawthorne you will receive the tools to help navigate your way through life. Our primary goal is to get you mentally stable enough to reenter society." There was an unspoken challenge in his eyes as he leaned forward and whispered, "I can't make any promises, though."

"I don't need your help." Each syllable was dripping with acid. I didn't know anything about Dr. Folton except that he was a doctor, and if his behavior was any indication, an asshole. He was just like the others—Judge Wexler, my attorney, and even my own mother. They all thought I had checked out, so to speak, and felt the only way to *check-me-back-in* was to have me committed. All because I told the truth about the wrong person: Joe.

"Most mentally ill people are not aware they're mentally ill." Dr. Folton stated on his way out the door. "Sometimes it takes more than a diagnosis for patients to see the big picture." Now in the hallway, he looked over his shoulder. "Do you have any questions for me before I get the nurse to escort you to your room?"

My emotions were all over the place. Part of me was thrilled that I had gotten away from Joe, and part of me was angry that he had escaped justice. He was probably at our six-bedroom estate, slumped back in his overstuffed recliner, sipping on a beer as he celebrated his victory and counted his millions. And I was here. *All because I told the truth.*

And where was Elizabeth?

Six feet under...

Because she had attempted to tell the truth.

When I didn't speak Dr. Folton walked away and Nurse Kline entered seconds later, a pair of black scrubs tucked under one arm. The last time I had seen her, her platinum blonde hair had been pulled into a tight bun at the top of her head, showcasing the enchanting bone structure of her heart-shaped face. But she'd since released the bun and her platinum curls were splayed out over her small shoulders. She didn't look a day over thirty and was gorgeous, reminding me of the pianist, Charlene, at the country club my mother always dragged me to every Sunday after church. "You're not going to make a run for it, again, are you?" she asked, squinting. "I cut you some slack last night because you weren't fully in the system yet, but if you run away again I will be forced to sedate you and place you in solitary."

Sedate me...for running? My eyes widened slightly at the thought of a giant needle ripping through the muscles of my butt. Taking the black scrubs from Nurse Kline I shook my head and murmured a pathetic, "No."

"That's what I thought."

Ten minutes later I found myself trailing behind Nurse Kline, dressed in the hideous scrubs that were deemed mandatory to separate us from medical personnel. Joe had drilled it into my mother's head early on that sophisticated women wore skirts and dresses, and my mother being the weak woman that she was, had conformed to his demands, making sure I'd followed that rule for the last eight or so years. Because of that I wasn't prepared for the fabric riding up my crotch as I made the dreaded walk-of shame through Hawthorne's main hallway.

"Keep up, Evans." Nurse Kline quietly scolded.

I took in the scene to make sure the coast was clear and tugged at the fabric hugging my crotch. "I'm not used to these pants." I said.

"Religious parents?"

I tugged at the fabric again, "Something like that."

Nurse Kline's face screwed-up but she didn't push the issue any further, and I immediately felt like an idiot for bringing it up in the first place. *Stupid…stupid…stupid.*

On my right wrist was a medical ID bracelet with my name, birthdate, current medications (none), and my room number. Seeing my information below HAWTHORNE ASYLUM was the cherry on top of an already crappy twenty-four hours.

"There are three floors at Hawthorne: Floor A, Floor B, and Floor C. Floor A is for patients with mild diagnosis'. Floor B is for patients with moderate to severe symptoms," Nurse Kline paused and peeked over her shoulder at me, "and Floor C is reserved for severe patients who could possibly be a danger to others or themselves.

You will be on Floor B."

How lovely….

Like yesterday, everything was white—the floors, walls, nurses' stations, nurses' scrubs. The only exception was a buff security guard, who was wearing his typical blue policeman garb. At the center of each patient door were room numbers. My heart started to really pound as we approached Room #19; the room I had sought refuge in last night. I had held onto hope for the last twenty minutes of Nurse Kline's "patient orientation" that Hannibal Sketcher and I would be on different floors. *That ship had sailed, apparently.*

Aside from his strange fascination with morbid sketches, I had no reason to despise Patient #19. But during my three or four minutes trapped in his room, I had shown weakness by fear. I could've remained calm and opened the door, set myself free, but I didn't. I'd elected to let the fear consume me, just as I had when my stepfather, Joe, went off on one of his rampages. The sad thing about it was Patient #19 hadn't been shouting at me, or throwing things—all he had been doing was walking toward me; a simple act that sent alarm bells going off in my head. *This really couldn't get any worse*...or could it?

Stopping at the nurses' station, Nurse Kline threw one arm to the right, "The right side of the hall is for male patients," her left arm flung to the left, "the left side is for our female patients. All patient doors must be open during the day at all times. You are not allowed to go into other patients' rooms without *their permission*." Nurse Kline stressed the last part. "If you are given permission to do so, you are not to touch anything inside of their room unless they tell you it is okay to do so. Personal space is very important around here, as you'll soon come to find out."

Okay. That seemed fair. I liked my personal space as much as the next person. My gaze shifted to the massive dry erase board nailed into the wall behind her. There were twenty-four numbers in numerical order, with dates and yellow stars in square boxes. I held back a snort, "What is that for?" I had an idea, but needed confirmation that I was about to be treated and rewarded like a five-year-old.

Nurse Kline glanced over her shoulder. "Oh that? That is the HP board." She looked back at me, "Every day, should you behave and participate, you will be awarded a star."

"Just like kindergarten..." I mused.

"Somewhat. But kindergarteners don't get to go home after a month of straight stars," She nodded at the HP board, "they do."

Home? I had been close to yawning, but was now suddenly intrigued with the childish yellow stars. Seeing the hope enter my eyes, Nurse Kline let out a heavy sigh. "You would only be allowed to get out for the weekend." she answered. "You would be allotted a two day pass to spend with your family."

Family…spend a weekend with the same family that had put me in here in the first place? Spend the weekend with Joe? Those stars represented freedom, but at what cost? My sanity? That was why I was in here in the first place, because everyone thought I had lost my mind…and the reward for gaining my mind would be losing it all over again? Seemed a little messed up from where I was standing.

The only good that would come from it would be getting to investigate, something I had wanted to do for six months, but hadn't been given the opportunity. After the murder Joe had put a dead-bolt on Elizabeth's bedroom door, preventing everyone, even my mother, from going inside. He claimed it was to make the transition easier, but I knew better. There was something in Elizabeth's old room that he didn't want anyone to see, *or find*. I just didn't know what.

Nurse Kline pointed at Patient #18 on the HP board. "That's you, Evans. #18. You can start collecting stars tomorrow."

You need to get in that room. I clenched my fists and nodded, my eyes falling to the floor beneath me. All I needed was one pass, one chance to rummage through Elizabeth's things for something the police might've missed.

And I was going to get it.

Oh yes...

And then Joe would get his.

"Alright." Nurse Kline clapped once, dragging me out of my thoughts. "I'll take you to your room and you can get settled in. I'm sure you want to get a little rest before your first day tomorrow."

My room was at the very end of the hallway—directly across from Hannibal Sketcher's. *Of course...* the fates weren't satisfied with my public humiliation from the previous day, so they'd made it their mission to remind me of said humiliation every day.

Rolling my eyes, I dragged my feet behind Nurse Kline, shaking my head at the irony of it all. I could've been #13 or #2, but no...

My room was small, around eight by ten feet, with white walls and one twin bed.

There were a few shelves nailed into the wall closest to the door to put my things in.

Whatever they allowed me to keep.

"Before I forget," Nurse Kline patted down her scrub top and pulled out a folded up note, "Here is your daily schedule. Part of your therapy requires getting in a routine. If you have any questions, come by the nurses' station."

I nodded. "Okay."

As per the rules, the door to my room was still open long after Nurse Kline had fled. I spent most of my first night pacing back and forth, getting used to my new surroundings. The true extent of Judge Wexler's punishment didn't come until they called lights out over the intercom and seconds later my door slammed shut. Anxious, I crawled into bed and briefly closed my eyes and attempted to relax, but the feeling was fleeting when my finger brushed across a piece of paper tucked underneath my pillow *Alright…remember to be calm, Evans.*

Yes. Be cool.

For all you know it could be trash.

Right.

Maybe the janitor had forgotten to toss it after the last patient was released. Yanking the piece of paper out from my pillow, I walked over to my door and squatted down.

There was a small crack of light, not a lot, but just enough to see what was on it.

Shit.

It wasn't trash.

But it sure as hell felt like it.

What I had originally thought was paper turned out to be a thick piece of parchment.

Sketch paper.

All of the wind was knocked out of me.

The strokes were so precise and drawn with a purpose. A girl, who bore a striking resemblance to me, was lying in front of a door, a sword shoved right through her chest. My hands began to shake.

Her mouth was barely open, blood spilling through the corners and down her neck. She was clothed—thank God —but that didn't make me feel any better. Her outstretched arms were reaching out to someone, something, which had obviously failed to help her. A lump formed in my throat and I tried to swallow it but couldn't. I felt cold and numb, laid bare for the entire world to see… and above all else, I felt weak.

FOUR

Laces

"WE'VE SPOKEN of this in the past, you and I, about how your good deeds might not be perceived in the same light as someone else's good deeds. I don't know why you gave her that sketch," Dr. Young said, pursing his lips, "and I'm not judging you the least bit for doing it, all I'm going to say is the next time you feel compelled to give a gift... *don't.*"

Oh Gambrielle...she had been at Hawthorne for less than forty-eight hours and had already violated our most sacred law: keep your mouth shut. You wouldn't rat out your supply source if you were busted for, say, cocaine, or tell the cops which bank you robbed. So why the hell Gambrielle felt it was necessary to show-off the masterpiece that I'd devoted a full hour to in solitary, only God knows. What was meant to be a kind gesture, a welcome gift—had turned into the Salem Witch Trials with yours truly at the center of it all. Dr. Young acted as though I had sacrificed a chicken to a wildfire and danced around with my bare ass out.

Dr. Young looked over his desk to where I sat slumped down in the seat reserved for his clients—my legs crossed, shoes propped on the edge of his desk. He shook his head in dismay and pinched the bridge of his nose, "Do you like solitary, Laces, is that it? Because I can designate a room specifically for you—three meals a day, no TV, no pretty little girls to flirt with."

"Are you serious…all because of a sketch?" I uncrossed my legs and quickly leaned forward, "You're the one always telling us to go the extra mile to make a newbie feel welcome, and the one time I do it you bitch because it doesn't meet your standards?"

Pffft. Rising to my feet, I pointed at the sketch splayed out on his desk like a treasure map, and specifically, to the sword slicing through her chest, "It was supposed to be symbolic!"

"Yes well, she didn't see it that way, I'm afraid." I cocked my head, "Well maybe she needs to clean the cum out of her eyes and take a second look!"

Dr. Young's head dropped, defeated. He let out a heavy sigh. "I have done everything in my power to help you—but you've given me no choice." He reached for the phone on his desk, "I'm going to have to call your father."

I scowled. This was ridiculous! The sketch wasn't even that morbid. Compared to the other sketches on my wall, it was definitely one of the tamer ones. "He put me in Hawthorne to get rid of me, and you think he's going to want to talk to you about me?" A strangled laugh broke through the air as I threw my head back, "That's rich!"

Dr. Young's finger shot up. "Hi, this is Dr. Young at Hawthorne Asylum. Is Mr. Caster available?"

Noooo, I mouthed. And he wouldn't be for a very long time. Ever since my mother passed four years ago, that man had made it his mission in life to avoid me like the plague. My father was the owner of Caster Industries—a company that manufactured hybrid vehicles—and spent every waking moment traveling the world, meeting with business partners and negotiating new deals, greasing the palms of the world's elite. He was a self-made man, a feat he used to enjoy bragging about at our family's annual Christmas party. With nothing more than a dream and two dollars to my name I built an empire from the ground up, he used to say with a boyish twinkle in his eyes. I hadn't spoken to my old man in six months. The last I'd heard he was in Paris.

"Do you know when he will be available?" Dr. Young asked, taking a deep breath and pinching the bridge of his nose. "Yes, I'll hold."

I leaned forward and whispered, "You're going to be holding for a while." If not forever.

A stare-down ensued. "I will hang up this phone right now if you apologize to Gambrielle AND show her around." Dr. Young bargained, twirling the cord around his index finger. "I had tasked Carrie Malone with showing her the ropes, but she got released yesterday."

"You mean like a tour guide?"

"I want you to give her some direction. She needs it right now." Before I could come up with a wiseass rebuttal, he reached for something under his desk, a newspaper, and holding the phone firmly between his cheek and shoulder, held up the Asheville Times like a shining beacon. "Going once, going twice…"

On the cover of the Asheville Times was a headline: DA EVANS' DAUGHTER AGREES TO PLEA DEAL; HAWTHORNE OFFICIALS CAN NEITHER CONFIRM NOR DENY HER PLACEMENT. A photo of Gambrielle sitting in a courtroom—hands clasped together, legs crossed, wavy brown hair styled to the nines

—came into view, and as much as I fought it, I couldn't control the shit-eating grin that settled on my face even if I tried. Turns out Little Miss Innocent wasn't so innocent after all.

"She might be a little hesitant at first to engage in conversation with you given all that's happened, but she'll move past it, I hope." He was referring to the sketches and fainting episode in my room. "Gambrielle has no idea what lies ahead, but you and your friends do." Dr. Young 's smirk now mirrored my own. "You guys know what it's like to be thrown away with all the cameras watching your every move. So, what do you say?"

The guys Dr. Young was referring to were Reyes Park, Varla English, and Thorne Walsh—the only three people at Hawthorne whose crazy matched my own. Varla had always complained about the toxic levels of testosterone in our group, so I was confident she would welcome the stray with open arms. Thorne and Reyes, however, would be a different story. Change wasn't exactly Reyes's strong suit, and Thorne hated everyone in general.

"The only direction I've ever given is to my cock…" I pointed out.

Dr. Young held up his palm. "I'm going to pretend I didn't hear that. Do we have a deal or not?" There was a bit of anger brewing in his eyes when he finally looked up at me. He had put up with a lot of my shit over the last two years, more than any therapist got paid to put up with, so I kind of felt I owed it to him. *Shit.*

"YOU HAVE to tell me every detail: what did the headline say? Did she become irate in court and make Judge Wexler take off his toupee?" The excitement in Varla's perky voice was contagious as she pushed her lunch tray down the line, picking only fruits and nothing else. Her bony hand pointed at a cup of sliced oranges, which the lunch lady happily handed her with no complaints. As long as it wasn't a food supplement protein shake, everyone was thrilled with her progress. Her black hoodie was starting to fill out and I could actually make out the word Legends across her chest now. Glancing through the bright blue locks curtaining her face, she asked, "Didn't you have Judge Wexler, Laces?"

I shook my head. "Judge Collins." The douchebag had teased me with weekly therapy sessions and a homebound program, the usual punishment for first-time offenders. But when judgement day finally came there wasn't a pastor in sight that could've saved me. Putting a salad bowl on my tray, I glanced over my shoulder, "Reyes?"

"Simmons." Reyes answered, moving his tray along. "The bastard wanted to send me to juvie, but my lawyer made a big stink about my supposed *asthma*," he made air quotes, "so they threw me in here."

"I had Wexler." Throne muttered, dragging all of our attention to where he stood a few feet back, snapping his fingers so the lunch lady would get the hint to pass along more butter for his potato. "Court lasted for two minutes. The bitch wanted me to fuckin beg for my freedom and shed a few crocodile tears." His words were clipped, purposeful. He shook his head resolutely. "I don't beg for shit."

Varla shot him a pointed look. "You begged for your meds last month while you were in solitary. "

Thorne gave her a hard, challenging look of his own. "I was mentally incapacitated, so that doesn't count." Nurse Kline had found his stash of liquor buried in a homemade Tortuga in the garden out back.

"Whatever. It'll be nice to have another girl around to help take care of you three." Varla said, and when Thorne shot her go-to-hell look, she added, "no offense."

No arguments there. Thorne, Reyes, and I were a bit of a handful, and it would be a nice change of scenery. But everyone was forgetting about the elephant in the room: Gambrielle was a fuckin' snitch.

And snitches couldn't be trusted.

At Hawthorne all you had was your word, and Gambrielle had shot hers straight to hell. Once we were at our usual table near the emergency exit, Reyes was already on top of it, ready to remind everyone of the travesty that was being overlooked.

"She ratted Laces out over a *sketch*..." His weary eyes searched everyone at the table, "Not a cigarette, not alcohol, but a *sketch*. And you guys want to roll out the welcome wagon? Hell no." He stabbed his fork into his potatoes and shook his head over and over, sputtering off something inaudible. "She could be a damn spy and the next thing you know our asses are in the new docu series about troubled teens."

Thorne and Varla had their reservations about certain things, but Reyes? Reyes had paranoia like no one else. I guess that's what happens when you try to kidnap your ex-girlfriend? According to Reyes, he didn't even get her into his trunk before seeing the blue and red lights coming toward him. What he had thought were fireworks turned out to be Charlotte's finest coming to haul his crazy ass downtown.

Reyes never spoke much about what had become known as *the incident*, but over the years I'd managed to glean a few things from our late-night conversations and pieced it together:

1. Reyes was in love with her.
2. They had picked out china patterns, so shit was serious.
3. Said girlfriend was unaware of his feelings, *or that he even existed*.
4. The stalking charges were dropped in exchange for being committed.

"Hey, no one said anything about rollin' out the welcome wagon." I said, tapping my palm against the table to rein in my crew. Reyes scoffed. "So she's a fuckin snitch, alright? I'm not denying that. But Dr. Young has done a lot for our asses," I paused, glancing at Thorne pointedly, "especially you."

Thorne rolled his eyes.

It was the same shit every time we elected to bring someone into our group. Most patients at Hawthorne were like loose rats chasing their next meal; they couldn't figure out left or right, where the hell they were going or what they were doing—which was part of the appeal and punishment of being in a psych ward.

None of us knew what it was like to be a scared rat roaming the halls because we'd been rescued early on before shit got real.

Outside of Hawthorne's walls we were known for the newspaper clippings, Nancy Grace interviews, or magazine articles that had been written about us. Everyone in the world thought we were a waste of DNA. Crazy.

But inside Hawthorne we were legends. The patients here didn't associate us with our symptoms or mental stability, unlike the judge or our parents. No. Here they envied us. They wanted to be us.

They wanted to fuck us.

To the patients at Hawthorne, we were royalty.

My eyes drifted to the oversized black hoodie that seemed to swallow Varla's tiny frame. The word LEGENDS was embroidered across the center in white bold letters. Varla wore it like a crown, as did the rest of us.

We were untouchable.

FIVE

Gambrielle
————————————

"You're allowed five minutes a day, mmmkay? Other patients at Hawthorne need a turn too. Wouldn't want to show favoritism, would we? No." The charge nurse on afternoon duty, Mrs. Davis, treated me as though I had a mental handicap. Her bright eyes were sympathetic as she passed the corded phone across the marble white counter that served as the nurses' station. She was old, well into her sixties, and her strangled, southern voice was oddly comforting. "Now you go ahead and tell me who you want to call and I'll put it right in for ya, okay?"

I offered her the kindest smile I could muster, given the circumstances. It wasn't her fault I was here, after all, it was Joe's, and I had to keep reminding myself of that little fact as I leaned forward and slowly whispered, "I don't know my attorney's number. Do you have that on file some-where?" Yes, I needed to speak with him. ASAP. Being confined to a room all day and force fed meds was one thing; Getting demonic sketches from Hannibal Sketcher was another thing altogether.

Nurse Davis fell back into her chair and shot me a

pitiful look, "Oh honey. You'll have to forgive Laces. He's not well."

I blinked twice. "Laces?"

"The room you ran into yesterday? That was Laces' room." She confided and then admitted, "I heard you mentioning something about a sketch to Nurse Kline."

"Maybe I was referring to someone else?"

"That's not likely." she said, smiling. "Laces is the only patient that sketches on this floor."

All I could do was force a tight smile and nod. Word clearly traveled fast around Hawthorne.

Nurse Davis leaned forward and whisper-shouted, "He once drew a photo of me hanging from the Eiffel Tower. I had no clothes on and my insides were spilling out into the Paris sky." Her voice was so uppity, like this was the biggest piece of gossip she would get to share all year. Seeing my stunned expression, she cleared her throat and bared her set of white dentures, "You have to find the beauty in the ugly. That's what my momma always used to say. Poo on the fact that my guts were hanging out. But the Eiffel Tower was sketched to perfection." As if recalling a memory, she closed her eyes and nodded, rocking back and forth in her chair, "Oh, it sure was."

"I don't doubt it one bit, BUT—your guts were hanging out—"

"—had a beautiful sky." She rambled on, "Laces was even nice enough to put me in my favorite polka dot dress. It was torn, of course, but I still smiled at them rags."

I looked to my left, then right, no one was around to witness this atrocity, thank God. My head snapped back to her, "about that phone call. Do you um…have my attorney's phone number—or is there someone I could speak to?"

Nurse Davis reeled herself back in from her musings

and I was back to being treated like a mentally handi-capped being. "You're only allowed to call the people you put on your approved list. Did you put your attorney on your list?"

Did I? I bit my lip as I thought back to yesterday and to the paperwork Malcolm had given me after we accepted the plea deal. Everything had happened so fast.

"Let me check in the computer, okay?"

I nodded and whispered a prayer at about the same time a thin, blue-haired pixie girl bounced past me, laughing like a clown on speed. Our eyes briefly met and there was something behind them, an unspoken secret as she skipped away in her oversized black hoodie and black scrub pants, chanting "He's coming for youuu..." in a perky, songstress voice.

"Excuse me?" I prompted. A shiver coursed through my spine as she continued to repeat the same phrase over and over, the words bouncing off of the walls and into my ears, taunting me. Who was coming? Had my stepfather sent someone? My heart had picked up a little speed and I could feel the beads of sweat breaking out across my fore-head as pixie waved at me.

"Oh, don't worry about her. The jury is still out on that one." Nurse Davis said, squinting at her computer screen. "Ah! Here we go! You approved Claudette Evans and Stacey Hargrove." *Shit.* No Malcolm.

Claudette Evans was my mother/Joe's bitch, and had testified against me at trial. She was Joe's faithful minion, an abuse victim suffering from Stockholm syndrome. Any conversation with her this early after my plea deal would've resulted in another argument, and possibly Joe hanging up the phone for her. Something he had been known to do in the past...

Stacey Hargrove had been my best friend since I was

three. We were like twins, always finishing each other's sentences and knowing what the other would say before she said it. Her parents had treated me like I was their own daughter, and we often vacationed in Charleston together during the summer. But since the allegations were made public there hadn't been much conversation. Like my step-father, Stacey came from blue-blood roots, and blue-bloods were known to take pride in their reputations almost as much as their bank accounts.

"I'll just dial your mother, alright? No need to get all flustered over something like this." Nurse Davis said, ripping the selection right out from under me. She dialed the number and passed me the corded phone. I didn't know what I was going to say to my mother. Thanks for putting me in here?

The call went straight to voicemail.

"You've reached the mailbox of District Attorney Joseph Evans." My hand began to shake before his last name was uttered through the receiver. "I'm unable to answer your call. Leave a message after the beep."

I quickly hung up the phone and jerked away, shaking my head repeatedly, "No. That's not right. It's the wrong number." I wanted to believe there had been a mistake during check-in, or confusion with whoever transferred the data to the computer.

Nurse Davis glanced back at her computer screen. "Huh, well that's strange. All of the numbers for your approved list are the same."

That bastard. Joe had taken away everything from me—my family, my future—and was now trying to wipe what was left of me clean off of this earth. The outrage I felt in that moment, the pain, aggravation...I swallowed the lump in my throat and handed back the phone. "Is there any way to get that changed?"

Nurse Davis' lips turned downward. "You were checked in involuntarily. Your power of attorney would have to meet with the office manager and make the adjustments."

Great.

Just perfect.

Fists clenched at the sides, I stormed off without saying another word. Never in my life had I thought about killing anyone. Stacey used to say I didn't have it in me, that sweet southern girls like me didn't kill, we buried. Girls like me were the ones always grieving the destruction of those around me. But I swear if Joe had walked through the metal double doors right then and there, I would've torn him apart limb by limb, and wouldn't have thought twice about it.

Clutching my right wrist to my chest, I squeezed hard as the image of me tied to my bed—starving and lying in my own waste—slammed into my mind. I'd been twelve the first time I endured his abuse. And all because of a B. I'd been expected to keep a perfect 4.0, but had slipped in math towards the end of the semester. My mother had hidden the report card in her purse and grounded me before Joe could have his say. I didn't like my punishment, but I'd dealt with it and went straight to my room after school for three days. Then, on the fourth day, I arrived home to find Joe sitting on my bed, report card in one hand, a long rope in the other. My mother had noticeably been absent, and the more I think about it now, I under-stand why. She knew what he was going to do and being the coward that she was, she didn't want to be around. It seemed like I was tied to my bed forever, instead of just three days. "You will learn, cunt." Joe had said once my frail body was free and staggering to the bathroom. "Until you start paying some damn bills around here, you'll do as I say!"

And until six months ago, I had obeyed his every command. I had catered to his every wish.

"Joe has an anger problem, I know. But nobody's perfect." My mother had once said. "He doesn't know how to express himself in the right way."

I had glared at her from the kitchen table as though she was crazy. Nothing about Joe's behavior was right, and because of her excuses I now had scars lining both of my wrists from where I had fought to break free from the ropes. "You need help, Mom." I had said in a serious tone. "I can call somebody! The police!"

But she would hear nothing of it. To my mother we were the lucky ones. We had a beautiful two story estate in a gated community, fancy cars, and the adoration of everyone around us. To her it was an even exchange: we endured Joe's sadistic ways and torture, and in return lived a life of luxury.

Maybe if she had spoken up years ago I wouldn't have ended up here, I thought as I slowly entered my room. It was a fool's notion, really, because my mother was the weakest one of all. She'd proved as much when she lied on the stand for him.

I was angry, miserable, and just wanted to sleep the rest of the day away, but little did I know there was a surprise in my room that awaited me. I had barely made it two feet into my room when I saw him:

Laces, A.K.A. Hannibal Sketcher, was lying on my bed.

SIX

Laces
_____

SYMPATHY, pity, empathy—these were words that didn't register in my dictionary, and I planned on keeping it that way.

This, what I was about to do, was nothing more than a favor—an exchange between enemies at war. For whatever reason Gambrielle had been misinformed about the rules of war, and to keep peace among my crew, I felt it was my duty as a citizen of Hawthorne to give her a quick lesson; a reminder of who she was fuckin' with.

I'd made myself comfortable on her bed—eyes closed, arms thrown behind my head, the scent of fresh roses attacking my nostrils—when I heard it: a soft gasp coming from the doorway.

Ah, showtime.

The sound of her feet shifting anxiously, and her fingernails digging into her porcelain skin, made my lips twitch.

I wasn't a total shithead; Every leader deserved their *Braveheart* moment before pulling out their sword, and I gave her that as a courtesy: she had a minute to collect herself and speak her peace—but instead chose to stand in the same spot, presumably the doorway, and cower like a bitch.

Fuckin' newbie…

"Word in the halls is my masterpiece offended your delicate sensibilities, milady." I said, cracking my eyes. Gambrielle was standing in the doorway, her brown eyes full of shock, fear, and disbelief. I swear I thought she was going to shit herself, *or maybe she already had*. Rising from the bed like a predator, I stalked toward her, hands clasped behind my back. "You have yet to speak. It's fuckin' insult-ing, and starting to piss me off."

"You're not supposed to be in here without my permis-sion." she said in a soft rush, and I couldn't help but chuckle. *Permission? Ha!* I was the judge, jury, and execu-tioner, she just didn't know it yet. *Oh, but she will…*

"Oh, I'm sorry, I thought since you already went into my room, *uninvited*, that I should extend the same courtesy." I said matter-of-factly.

"I…I…I don't. I mean…"

What's this? I craned my neck forward to try to make sense of her stutters. Her voice was soft, low, like that of a choir girl. It only fueled my aggravation.

"I…run…you." She tapped her chest. "I…r-rrrran to…"

Yeah, *no shit, you ran your fuckin' mouth*—is what I wanted to say to her caveman rambles, but she quickly gathered herself and pointed a sharp manicured nail my way, surprising even me. "I know your kind, how your brain works!" She hissed, eyes still as wide as ever. "Just stay away from me, Hannibal Sketcher! Understand? Stay away!"

The only thing missing was a cross and holy water and we would've had a full-blown exorcism. And you know what? It was about damn time. This was the reaction I'd been waiting for.

Reyes was right: I had experienced a moment of weakness in my room when I cut a piece of her hair, and that type of behavior was no good at Hawthorne. The people here didn't sweep shit like that under the rug, they exploited it. Just like Gambrielle exploited my sketch for her own gain.

"Hannibal Sketcher." I repeated, seeing how it tasted on my tongue. "That's very original. Did you come up with it all on your own, or were you under the influence?" *of meds…*

Her eyes drew into slits. "Whatever this is let's get it over with. I'm exhausted and just want to go to bed." She muttered. She had a little bite left in her bark, not much, but some, and thought it would be enough to take me on.

She was *wrong*.

"You've disappointed me." I said, enclosing the distance between us. Now inches away from her lips, I kept my eyes trained on hers and pushed an auburn curl off of her shoulder. She shivered. "I thought you were going to be a good girl, but you ran your mouth, stray—tsk, tsk…"

She stood her ground, swatting my smooth hand away like a fly. "Yes, I did." The pride in her voice was unmistakable as she poked the center of my hard chest and added, "Your sketch was horrid and inappropriate. The only place it belongs is in the trash." She probably had a lot more she wanted to say—oh, I don't know, like how I reminded her of an 80's on-screen serial killer—but I didn't give her the chance. My eyes fell to the spot on my chest, and to the spot where mere seconds ago her finger had been. I could still feel the nerves throbbing from the indention the nail had left upon impact. What fucks I had left—which admittedly wasn't a lot, maybe one or two—jumped ship and forgot to throw me a life vest. *Bye-bye, Gambrielle*.

"Was that a cry for help, or did you piss the wrong man off?" I asked, a little too casually.

Confusion filled her brown hues. "What are you talking about?"

"Oh, you heard me." I taunted. My eyes zeroed in on the scars on her wrists, and specifically, the initials. A harsh chuckle vibrated through my chest. "I didn't know branding was a thing, but to each his own." As the recognition finally hit home, all-of-the-color drained from her face and I lunged forward and grabbed her wrist. Her soft skin burned against mine as I traced the welts of the initials and flashed her a sinister smirk, "Pity. You had such beautiful skin."

Zero fucks…

That was all it took to bring the inner bitch out of her.

"Enough!" She jerked once, twice, trying to break free of my hold and failed.

My fingers tightened around the already sensitive flesh and I squeezed hard, bringing her to her knees. Her lips formed the shape of an O and tears pooled into her eyes, but she didn't scream. The bravery she had displayed before was now gone and had been replaced with true fear. *Good girl.* Her chest rose and fell like she had run a marathon, her bloodshot eyes crippling as I slowly leaned forward and whispered into her ear, "I'm just getting started. This is my domain. Do you understand?" She gave a quick nod, but I wasn't satisfied. "Answer me!"

"Your domain." She whispered, not meeting my gaze.

"That's right. My domain. If you have a fuckin' problem, you take it up with the *king*. Not the servants. Understand?"

She nodded.

In the midst of my *Braveheart* moment, I took a deep breath to rein myself back in and wished I had suffocated. The sweet smell of roses was back and more potent than ever, repelling off of her neck like toxic fumes. *Fuck.* I was too close and having a hard time finding the willpower to stay away. Squeezing my eyes shut, I cursed. Her smell truly was intoxicating.

And then, something unexpected happened: she took a fistful of my black hoodie and pulled herself up, drawing me close, her body shivering against mine as she leaned her cheek on my chest and whispered, "Help me ."

"Humm.."

"Help me, please!"

My body turned to stone. I blinked.

Okay this is not…what is happening here? My eyes darted to the empty hallway, then back to her hair which was now tickling my neck. "What are you doing?" I whispered, frowning. "Get off of me, now." Damn vixen.

Gambrielle released my hoodie, and for a split second I thought Braveheart was back and ready to fight to the death.

Well, make a few threats and maybe slap her ass around…

But no.

Completely ignoring my demands, the bitch wrapped her arms around my back and snuggled up to the hollow of my chest. My jaw dropped. *What kind of witchcraft is this?* After everything I had just done, she wanted to *cuddle*?

"You're warm." She whispered into my chest. "And you smell like wintergreen and charcoal."

"I smoke."

"Mmmm." She hummed approvingly.

"It's a mixture of the charcoal I use for my sketches, and cigarettes." I explained.

My hands had fallen to my sides and taken cover in my pants pockets—where I prayed they remained. Feeling a bit confused about the sudden change of events, I started to pull away, but she tightened her grip around my waist and mumbled something that sounded like no.

Truth be told, part of me didn't want her to let go. There was something strangely comforting in the way the stray held my waist and rocked side to side, as though we were dancing. It was like we were in our own little world, away from everything, and all of the problems that seemed so important only moments ago, vanished.

"You're mommy's little bumblebee. Mommy's little bumblebee." Gambrielle started humming a few verses and pushed onto her tiptoes, she whispered into my ear, "help me."

My brows furrowed. "I can't." I whispered, breathless.

I had no idea what she needed help with, but whatever it was, the answer would have to be no. I could barely help myself, let alone a stranger. *But this feels…what is the word*? Content? No. Calm? Relaxed? Peaceful? I couldn't figure it out. It felt good though, real good, her arms holding on to me for dear life. "My mother smelled like roses." I whispered, resting my cheek on top of her head. I closed my eyes and gave in to it. "We had a garden in the front of our house and every Sunday she would pick a few and put one in my room."

"Smelled like roses? As in past tense?"

"Mmm. She die—"

"—Lincoln."

My eyes flew open at the sound of his voice—I glanced over my shoulder.

Well fuck…

Thorne was standing in Gambrielle's doorway, muscular arms crossed, and an amused look on his face.

Thrown over his shoulder was a Legends hoodie, which made the moment even more awkward and confusing for me. "We took a vote." Thorne said, smirking at Gambrielle —who was mortified and quickly released me.

Shit. I held up my hands. "I didn't touch her."

Thorne snorted.

"The one time I am innocent and no one is going to believe me." I said, rolling my eyes. I put some serious distance between me and the stray. Like ten feet. It would've been more, but beggars couldn't be choosers in a twelve-by-twelve room. "What's with the hoodie?"

"We took a vote." Thorne said again. Jerking the hoodie off of his shoulder, he threw it to Gambrielle, who dodged it, and explained, "Varla showed Rey her tits and he became a democrat."

Noooooo! For the third time that day, my mouth dropped in pure disbelief!

No.

Her joining our group sounded good coming from Dr. Young, BEFORE she decided to become Miss Cuddles and infringe upon my oxygen.

"Thank you, but… I'm going to have to decline the offer." Gambrielle said, holding her head up high. It shocked the hell out of me and Thorne. "I don't need any help, okay? All I want to do is get out of here and serve my own personal justice." Her lips drew into a thin line as the same bravery from earlier reentered her soul. Turning to me, she said, "I'm sorry about the sketch, reporting it I mean. It was out of character for me and very rude."

It was like someone had punched me in the face. Even the way she apologized somehow managed to come off insulting.

"Personal justice? What are you going to do? Kick someone out of your country club?" As if preparing for prayer, I clasped my hands together in front of my chest and gazed up at the white ceiling. "Oh God, please don't! Don't take away the Stepford Wives and macaroonsssss!" I proclaimed dramatically, drawling out the s. Pointing a sharp finger at the ceiling, I continued, "Take the damn Porsche, the kids, the Hampton Estate—but you leave my fuckin' macaroons alone! Do you hear me?"

Thorne threw his head back and laughed.

But Gambrielle didn't, which was the intended effect. She stood, mouth agape, cheeks flushed, probably feeling like an idiot when I shifted my attention back to her. "Oh I'm sorry, was that rude?" I asked, pouting. "Oops, that was out of character for me. Normally I'm not like that."

Laces 1, Gambrielle 0.

After that, she wasted no time rushing to the door. She extended her arm and said, in a proper tone, "As much as I've enjoyed this conversation, I must retire."

"This is 2020. Not the 1700s. That shit might've worked in Heathcliff's day, but not here." I said, stepping through the doorway and into the hall. Thorne followed behind, still snickering about the macaroons.

Gambrielle performed an awkward wave that resembled more of a salute. "Nice of you to drop in. Goodnight."

And because I was, well, an asshole, and to further drive my point home, I held out my arms and bowed like a servant, "Until next time, milady."

"There won't be a next time." She seethed.

Now in the hallway I stood straight, my dark hair catching in my eyes as I flashed a cocky grin. "We'll see about that."

SEVEN

Gambrielle

Day 1

A LOUD BANG came at my door early the next morning, drawing me out of a deep sleep.

"Rise and shine! This is your thirty minute warning! If you want a shower ladies and gents you better get up!" The man's voice was deep, loud, and full of authority. He banged on my door two more times before unlocking it and turning the lights on, "Up! Up! Up!"

He didn't look like the typical security guard; he was short, maybe 5'3, with a balding head that was too big for his thin body. The blue security guard uniform practically swallowed him whole. "My name is Winston and I'll be looking after you for the remainder of your stay," There was a brief pause, "did you hear me, Evans? It's time to get up and greet the day! Come on girl, let's move, move, move!" Each move ended with a clap.

I groaned and threw my arms over my face to shield my eyes from the light. "Go away!"

"Don't make me drag your little butt out of that bed." Winston sounded like he was joking now, but still. After the day I'd had yesterday, I didn't think it was too much to ask for another hour of rest.

Not that I got it anyway.

The second my eyes started to drift shut, Winston was right beside me, jerking the covers off of the bed and tossing them across the room. CLAP. "Up." Another clap. "Up!" A third clap. "Up!"

Twenty seconds later Winston was shouting again, except this time it wasn't directed toward me. "It's time to get up, Laces! Morning meds in thirty, my friend!" I rolled over on my side and cracked my eyes to see Winston flipping Laces' light switch on-and-off several times. I was dog tired and drained of any feeling in my limbs, but even I couldn't suppress the chuckle that passed through my lips at the sound of Laces fierce battle-cry, "Get. The. Fuck. Out!"

"Are you going to get up?" Winston demanded.

"Yes."

"When?"

"When I damn well feel like it!" Laces bellowed, pulling the covers over his head. Winston remained at the side of his bed, hands on his hips. Laces, dull and tired grumbling obscenities emerged seconds later in the form of a threat, "If you don't leave I'm going to tell Kline you sexually assaulted me in the ear."

"You mean rear."

Laces uncovered his head and glared up at Winston, "No, ear. That puny thing you call a dick would be a disgrace for any asshole."

Sweet baby Jesus…

He didn't know when to quit—and honestly, I'm not sure he even knew how. I had to give props to Winston; he took his mental beating better than I did. Even with his manhood being savagely ripped apart, Winston still continued his duty, behaving as if nothing was amiss. I, however, had succumbed to Laces' attack and become another one of his victims. And in doing so Laces had gotten exactly what he wanted, a submissive. *Stupid.*

"I'm going to be back in five minutes." Winston warned. "And when I return your ass best be out of this bed, *or else.*"

That was the moment my tail got a voice of its own and forced me out of my twin bed. Scrub pants and top in one hand, beige slip-ons in the other, I rushed out of my room before Winston could finish his final room checks.

"Did you call my mom? Is she dead?" A young man wailed as I approached the nurses' station. Nurse Davis was holding his hand and trying to give him words of encouragement, but he was having none of it. He grabbed both of Nurse Davis' arms and pulled her close, his blood-shot eyes full of panic, "I flipped the switch eighty times like the voices said! You need to call her! What if they didn't keep their word?"

"Peter, shhh."

Peter's eyes flickered to me as I passed by, "Can you call my mom?"

Must find the showers quickly! I picked up my pace as Peter let out another wail of agony. Everyone was roaming the halls like zombies—bags under their eyes, arms held straight out, guiding them to wherever they were going. The showers were strategically placed near the cafeteria; some patients chit-chatted in the showers next to me, gossiping about this week's solitary victims, the lunch menu, and the weekly movie that was being shown in the entertainment room later today.

I spent twenty minutes scrubbing my entire body. It

seemed like no matter what I did, I couldn't get clean enough. I wanted rid of Joe, of all the scars lining my arms and legs. The soap bubbles briefly covered the scars and for a few seconds I felt normal, like how I had felt before Joe came into our lives. *Happy*. Then it came time for me to rinse…and a familiar dread entered my stomach as the soap bubbles washed away and the scars reappeared.

"You must behave today, remember that." I told myself while drying off.

Today was the beginning of my quest to get out of Hawthorne—my first full day at the asylum. If I could make it through today, unscathed, then I would have nine days to go.

After I finished my shower and got dressed, I pulled out the schedule Nurse Kline had given me the previous day.

7:00 am: Morning check.
7:15 am: Line-up at nurses' station.
7:30 am: Breakfast.
8:30 am: Community group.
9:10 am: Meet with Psychiatrist Dr. Young. (Tuesday's & Thursday's)
12:30 pm: Lunch
1:00 pm: Vital signs taken.
2:00 pm: Recreational therapy
4:00 pm: Visitation hour. (Sundays only)
5:00 pm: Line-up for dinner.
8:00 pm: Closure group.
9:00 pm: Night Meds.

Recreational therapy? Community Group? Closure Group? There were a lot of group activities we were required to participate in, and a tiny ounce of fear shot through me at the thought of having to endure all of the groups with Laces.

I was staring at my pale, plain reflection in the bathroom mirror, trying to towel dry my hair, when I heard her perky voice: "Gambrielle, right?"

My eyes flickered over my shoulder, to where the blue-haired pixie girl from yesterday stood a few feet away; "*He's coming for you*" replayed in my mind as she took the sink beside me and let out a kind smile. "Gambrielle?"

I forced a smile and nodded. "Yes."

She pulled out her brush and started combing her wet, blue hair; her eyes never leaving mine as she said, "I'm Varla. Varla English."

I put my towel down. "Gambrielle Evans." I said in a low voice.

"Oh, I know who you are." She cocked her head toward me and whispered, "I stole Nurse Kline's phone for a few hours and youtube'd your trial."

My eyes fell. "Oh." I didn't want to sound so disappointed, but I couldn't help it. Like everyone else in this godforsaken town, she probably thought I was a lunatic for trying to take my stepfather, the freakin' District Attorney, down.

Turning to face me, Varla leaned her hip on the sink and sighed. She was thin, too thin, and because of that her eyes were larger than normal. "I know you're pissed that you're here, and you'd rather suffer in silence, BUT...we're going to be friends." She proudly stated.

I had just gathered my clothes in my arms and my body came to a screeching halt. "You don't know me." I said awkwardly.

She gave me a pointed look, "Anyone that can stand in front of Judge Wexler and tell him to *kiss her ass* is pretty cool in my book. Plus, Thorne said you shot Laces down last night. Extra brownie points."

Her words shouldn't have cheered me up, but they did. "I'm not normally like that, but he kept interrupting me." I explained, flushing. Everyone knew Judge Wexler was a bastard.

"Maybe that's why his wife divorced him?" Varla offered. She'd turned back around to the mirror and was in the process of contouring her cheeks. "It was either that or his toupee."

We chuckled.

"Five minute warning!" Winston called from outside the women's shower room. "Hurry up and get in line for meds ladies! You know the drill!"

Varla closed her compact. "OMFG—can't even take a piss around here without the police brigade standing guard!"

"I heard that!" Winston called back.

"I meant for you to!" Varla shouted. Grabbing a black hoodie out of her bag she threw it on, the word Legends proudly displayed on her chest. She showed me the hamper to dispose of my dirty laundry, then we set off to get in the med line.

Dr. Folton hadn't spoken of meds during our short visit the previous day, so I didn't know what I was getting into when I took my place at the end of the line. Varla stood behind me, and as the first meds were distributed to eagerly awaiting patients, she whispered into my ear, "do you want to take the meds…or no?"

Bewildered that she would even hint at what she was hinting at, I slowly peered over my shoulder and whispered, "Well yeah, that's what they want us to do. I need to get a star." *I need to go home.*

Varla made a sad face. "I understand, I do, but…." She

lowered her voice to barely a whisper, "those meds make you a zombie. It's just not worth it, ya know?"

"I'll take my chances." I said, looking forward. If getting a pass home meant sacrificing my dignity, I would do it in a heartbeat. Joe needed his big day in court and I was going to deliver it. *Amen, amen.*

Laces was near the front of the line in deep conversation with two other patients, both guys. The first guy was shorter than his friends, but taut, and had lean muscles that flexed with even the slightest movement and dark, silky brown hair.

Varla nonchalantly pointed at the first guy, "That is Reyes Park."

And the second guy was…a beast. Period.

A monster.

He was like a blonde Tarzan. Long, blonde hair hung in a ponytail down his muscular back, except for a few light strands that had been tucked behind his ear. Outside of Hawthorne one would've thought he was a Marine, or at the very least a police officer. He had that look of authority, the look Winston was missing.

"And the one who looks like he could take down this entire floor is Thorne Walsh." Varla said.

The blonde Tarzan listened to his friends, but didn't converse with them. He seemed bored by the activity he was about to partake in and had zoned off into a crack in the tile floor. Reyes, on-the-other-hand, seemed to eat up everything Laces dished out and made it a point to maintain eye contact.

The first one to take meds was Reyes. The nurse slid a tray across the nurses' station with a small cup of water and three pills. He picked up the first pill and glanced at Varla, who casually wiggled a few fingers in his direction.

He winked, then tapped his finger against the water cup, twice, before tossing the pill into his mouth.

"You might want to look away." Varla whispered into my ear seconds later. "Things can get really messy."

I did a double take, "Messy? It's just a pill—"

I didn't even have the entire sentence out before Laces abruptly broke rank and took a mighty swing at poor, wailing Peter, who didn't see it coming. When Laces' fist connected with Peter's jaw, a gush of thick blood sprayed into the air, coloring the ceiling and walls a bright shade of crimson. A sea of black scrubs took cover behind the nurses' desk to shield themselves.

My hands flew to my cheeks. "Oh my God, what are you doing?" I screamed. Not that anyone could hear me. Those who hadn't taken cover behind the nurses' station had formed a betting pool off to the side and were swapping tens and twenties with Reyes. "Park, put me down for eighty on Laces!" A guy called out.

Reyes had whipped out a cell phone and was typing bets out as fast as he could. "What's your bet, Malone?" He asked.

Malone, a short chubby guy, appeared to be in deep thought as he counted out his twenties. "Eighty says Laces puts him in a coma!" He finally proclaimed, slapping his money into Thorne's awaiting hand nearby. Malone pointed at Thorne, and then Reyes, "I want the full report this time, none of that discharge shit and whatnot."

Reyes gave a curt nod, signaling that he understood Malone's conditions, then leaned to the side and flexed two fingers for the next better to step forward. "Next, come on keep it moving!"

With my hands still glued to my cheeks, I shook in my head in horror as Varla's bony arm wrapped around my waist and pulled. Where was the medical staff? Nurse

Kline? Security? Everyone was conveniently missing in action. "No, Varla! We have to help him!" I screamed. Even though we were in a psych ward, my first instinct was to demand for someone to call an ambulance.

"He's a lost cause, forget about him!" Varla insisted.

I gaped over my shoulder. "Someone needs to call security and 911!"

Varla remained her bubbly self as she reached into her black scrub top and retrieved a stick of gum. "Do you want to half it?" She asked, unphased by the chaos erupting around us.

"What? No!"

"Sorry, Reyes was supposed to get me some more but there was a shortage at the gift shop or something." She shrugged. "Never send a man to do a woman's job, right?"

The fight lasted for a total of ten minutes, but it felt like hours. By the time security arrived Peter had been beaten to a pulp, and Laces, Reyes, and Thorne had already tidied themselves up and joined everyone else back in line.

When asked who had wounded him, Peter refused to name the perpetrators, as did everyone else—myself included. I felt bad for Peter. No matter what he did, nothing justified the beating he took that day. *Nothing*. But at the same time I also couldn't justify spending the rest of my life eating through a straw all because I took up for Peter.

Nope.

So when my turn rolled around to speak with Winston, I played dumb. *Fight? Who? What? When?* Laces was watching me the entire time, waiting for me to roll over and tattle, just as I had with the sketch. His blue eyes taunted me, urging me to cross the line just so he could have his shits and giggles again.

I don't think so, douchebag.

As for my morning meds, Nurse Kline gave me three pills—one blue, one yellow, and one white. I wasn't told what they were for or their names. All I knew was I had to take those pills or lose a day. So I popped all three into my mouth, took a big sip of water and swallowed.

God help me...

EIGHT

Gambrielle

I DON'T REMEMBER MUCH about my first breakfast at the ward. Somewhere between lining up in rows of two and being herded to the cafeteria like sheep, the medication I'd been forced to take kicked in, and boy did it kick in hard.

My nose was on my face, but I couldn't feel it. At first I chalked it up to fatigue, maybe I was drained from lack of sleep and dealing with the aftermath of everything going on. But then things started moving, like spoons and forks, and I became surprisingly calm for no reason at all.

Where are my teeth?

I glided my tongue in my mouth and tried to feel around.

"Don't worry about it. It'll wear off." Varla assured me. She pushed two trays through the breakfast line, one for me and one for her. I couldn't feel my fingertips. "If you had been here the first time they made Reyes take his meds, ha!" she threw her head back and laughed, "let's just say you wouldn't feel so bad about your current state." Covering the side of her mouth, she leaned in and whispered, "Reyes thought he was Batman. Car, mansion, women—the whole nine yards. He even demanded to know where Alfred was!"

I craned my neck back and gaped up at her as best I could. *Whatttt?*

"Oh yesss! He wanted his rich boy keys, a suit—" She paused and gave me a serious look, "—the suit had to be Armani. He said the bat couldn't wear that cheap off the rack shit."

I didn't care about Reyes' Batman moment. There were more pressing matters to attend to, like my tongue—which had somehow forgotten how to go back in my mouth!

Varla picked out yogurt and some fruit for herself, while I stuck to pancakes and eggs—it seemed like a safe bet given my current state. By the time we reached the table I was starving. And that was a problem, you see, because I couldn't feel my fingertips. *Stupid meds.*

I stared at the plate of buttery goodness for two whole minutes before going rogue and dipping my face into the plate like an animal. If I'd been home and acted like this, Joe would've tied me up for a week, if not longer, and beat me with a belt.

"You need some help?" Varla offered. She reached for my fork, but I shook my head. No, all I wanted to do was eat so I could regain my strength and concentrate on getting out of Hawthorne.

Five minutes into my "caveman feeding" I heard, rather than saw, someone sit down across from me. "Damnit Varla! What are you staring at—get her face out of her fuckin' plate!" The man's voice sounded familiar *and pissed*. A smooth, warm hand dipped underneath my forehead and quickly pulled my face out of the buttery goo.

Chin, cheeks, and nose dripping in syrup, my head fell back, like a rag doll, and I stared up at the man who had rescued me from an almost certain death via affixation by pancake. *Well, well, what do we have here?* Blue eyes, sunkissed skin, taut features....from upside down my rescuer looked pretty damn fine.

"Hey, I tried!" Varla piped in. "If you had waited another minute to punch Peter, I might've had a better opportunity to persuade her to ditch the meds!"

"If you hadn't been so worried about your clown make-up you would've taken care of business!" My rescuer seethed.

Varla's mouth popped open. She rose from her seat like an exotic bird that had just spotted her next meal. Pointing a sharp red nail in his direction, she demanded. "You take that back right now, Laces!" They were like brother and sister with their feuding. "I worked really hard on contouring my nose today! You keep my face out of this!"

I didn't have the patience or concentration to be aggravated by his presence. Not when I was high as a kite. Laces could've been a serial murderer looking for his next victim, and I wouldn't have thought twice about it. *The power of meds...*

Laces picked up a napkin and attempted to dab at my dripping chin. "Just help me fix this before someone sees what's going on!" He demanded, and Varla folded her arms in defiance. They were at a standoff, neither giving an inch. Then Laces leaned toward her and whispered, "Do you want Dr. Folton getting handsy with your new friend? Hmm?"

"Handsyyyyy?" I slurred, frowning.

Varla's eyes fell.

"That's what I thought. Now help me clean her up."

Laces took care of my syrup facial while Varla fixed my hair as best she could. It wasn't the breakfast I envisioned for myself—the sticky hair, fingers, and face—but at least I didn't starve. I was still feeling the awful side effects when the cafeteria orderly announced that it was time for community group.

"Nooo." I groaned, rubbing my temples. "Just take me to my roommm." Let me sleep it off, I would be as good as new tomorrow.

"Can't do that, stray." Laces said, dipping down to eye level. There was a roughness to his voice, but I thought I heard a hint of kindness hidden somewhere between the syllables. Maybe he felt sorry for my struggle? His warm arm wrapped around my back and he carefully started pulling me to my feet. Our bodies were crushed together—his rock-hard chest pressed to mine, our eyes haphazardly observing each other's every move. His smell was musky and strong, with a pinch of wintergreen and darkness, which seemed to attack my scrub top, burying his scent deep into the fabric.

"Why are you doing this?" I mumbled, throwing my arm around his neck. In doing so I felt his dark, silky hair brush against my knuckles. The steady, rhythmic beat of his jugular vein throbbing against my palm as the blood passed through it was comforting in some sick and twisted way. My forehead creased.

Warm.

Peaceful.

Laces pressed his lips to my ear, sending a shiver coursing through my body.

"Because I owe Dr. Young, and you're going to owe me, stray."

I jerked my head away from his warm breath so fast, almost knocking both of us out with my delayed reaction.

"Owe you what?" I grumbled like a child. The meds were attacking my senses full force, but I still had some wits about me, thank God.

We started to move, arms-to-backs, toward the cafeteria exit. With the exception of a few patients being forced to eat from a straw, everyone else had already raced to where community group was being held. At least I have this going for me, I thought, fewer witnesses to testify to my shame of allowing Hannibal Sketcher to take care of me.

Once we'd made it safely to the hallway, Laces' mouth was back at my ear, his words a dark promise. "I haven't thought about what you're going to owe me, but don't worry, I'll think of something."

"I'm not having sex with you!" I all but spit out as we passed the nurses' station. Laces mumbled something to the nurse on duty about assisting me for the day, and despite her reluctance and curious eyes pinned on our physical contact, she said nothing and allowed us to move along, no questions asked.

My eyes widened. *No, hey you! Can't you see I need your help!*

"This may come as a shock, stray, but you're not exactly my type." Laces smoothly said once we were ten feet away, and I damn near tripped. *What?!* It was in that moment, right there, staggering past the bathrooms with drool dripping from my lip, that I realized I was in a lot of trouble. A LOT. Because instead of feeling relieved by his casual dismissal, I was disappointed.

Which made absolutely no sense at all. His favorite pastime involved sketching butchered women, for crying out loud.

"I like my women submissive, quiet, and obedient." Laces did a slow perusal of me and grinned, "And you are none of those things. Pity."

"Lucky for me."

"Lucky for you." Through the corner of my eye I caught a glimpse of Laces twirling a strand of my hair around his index finger. The mesmerized look in his eyes when he bent his finger and watched the auburn curl strain against his skin, like it was a precious jewel that needed twenty-four-hour security surveillance, left me reeling. I wasn't sure if I should get a restraining order, or swoon…

Damn.

Maybe Judge Wexler was right? Maybe I really did need help?

And it was that thought that brought everything to a head and forced me to take a good hard look at the path I was going down. Laces was attractive. There was no denying that. However, his favorite pastime involved sketching dead women—which was a deal breaker in my book. No one, not even Mr. Depp, could justify sketches like that and still maintain his *sexiest man alive* title.

Nope.

Dropping my arm from his shoulder, I gave Hannibal Sketcher's taut body a hard push and staggered toward the door labeled **COMMUNITY GROUP**. The drugs were still flowing strong, but I was feeling a little bit more in control than I had been. "This doesn't change anything!" I proclaimed over my shoulder. "You're still an 80's serial killer— *wannabe*—with an infatuation for butchering women!!!" *That's right…*

Hands clasped behind his back, he came to a dead stop a few feet behind me and said, "Do you have any idea what I just saved you from?" He looked over one shoulder, then back at me, eyes lit with rage. "I did you a big favor back there, and I generally don't do favors unless my dick is involved."

I waved him off with an unsteady hand. Yes, he was truly gorgeous, but he had a messed-up mind which really took the hot meter down to negative three. I had just reached the community group door and was preparing to open it when Laces snaked in front of me. His dark, narrow eyes had a sinister glow that made me shiver. He propped his hand against the door and held it shut to keep me from getting inside. "Dr. Folton likes to experiment with his scalpel after giving it to someone in the ass." he said in a sarcastic tone. "I've seen girls come out bleeding in places you wouldn't imagine—necks, arms, thighs—he likes to make his own entrance."

Oh God.

"You're making that up." I whispered, flushing. Looking at him head on was too distracting, so I glanced away. "I've already been alone with Dr. Folton and nothing happened so…"

"That you know of."

"Are you trying to scare me? Newsflash: it's not going to work." I glanced back at him and plastered the sweetest smile across my face. "I've spent the last eight years living with the devil reincarnated. If I can survive him, I can survive anything. NOW MOVE."

Laces didn't immediately obey my order. His hand remained firmly planted on the door while his curious eyes searched mine, looking for some type of answers, but finding none. Which was the way I liked it. The less he knew, the better. "The devil doesn't have shit on this place. He wouldn't last a week." I thought I saw sympathy flicker in his gaze as he dropped his hand and stepped away, but that would've been a foolish notion. People like Laces didn't embody that particular feeling.

Keeping true to my southern roots and good manners, I mumbled my thanks, opened the door and squeezed inside. Laces followed behind shortly after.

No more meds.

No.

Not after today.

The community room resembled a typical high school classroom; fifteen desks were evenly divided in three rows and aimed at a clean whiteboard. Motivational posters hung all over the walls, along with help ads and 1-800 numbers. A teacher's desk was off to the side; a young woman, smiling ear-to-ear occupied it.

The young woman put her hand to her chest, "I'm Miss Maroon. I'll be your advisor for community group." She nodded at the desks, "you can sit anywhere you like Miss…"

"Evans." I said. "Gambrielle Evans."

She wrote my name down on the yellow legal pad on the corner of the desk. "Great. Please take a seat so we can get started."

Varla waved from the back row and gestured for me to sit beside her. I obliged, taking the seat to her right. The two guys that had been standing with Laces prior to the fight, Reyes and Thorne, took up the two seats to Varla's left.

And, of course, Laces sauntered into the room like a runway model—earning him a few whistles and claps from the ladies in the front rows. Baring his pearly whites, he made his way to the back and parked his gorgeous derrière in the seat right beside me. Dumbfounded by his behavior, I slowly turned to face him. "Stalker much?" I whispered, stunned at this sudden turn of events.

Laces slouched back in his seat, flashed me a sexy grin, then gestured toward my face. "Is that syrup or drool coming off of your chin right there?"

My jaw set. *Syrup, probably*. Feeling dizzy, I swiped at my chin and turned to face the whiteboard. Miss Maroon was now standing in front of her desk, arms clasped behind her back. "Alright guys. Let's talk about last night. How did you sleep?" she asked. Her eyes scanned the room, waiting for someone to offer up a little insight.

A few patients mumbled their complaints, but the general consensus was pure silence.

Miss Maroon began pacing back and forth. "Raise your hand if you had a nightmare."

A few raised their hands.

"Nightmare's cannot hurt you. They aren't real." Miss Maroon said, as she met the gazes of those in the front row. "You have no control over your sleep, but you have control over yourself during the day. So let's make some excellent goals for today, alright? Let's combat fear with success." Opening a filing cabinet near her desk she retrieved a red notebook and handed it off to a patient in the front row, "Pass that to Gambrielle, please. Gambrielle, we write in our journals every morning. We keep track of our nightmares, sleep quality, struggles, and more importantly, our goals. At the end of the day we'll revisit the goals we have set each morning and see if we've accomplished them." She waited for my notebook to reach me before continuing with the discussion. "Everyone go ahead and write down your goals for the day. Please remember to be REALISTIC." Her eyes shot to Thorne. "Winning a million dollars and hiring a harem of exotic strippers is not realistic, Thorne."

Thorne rolled his eyes and dropped his head back. "Way to kill a dream, Maroon."

"If eating is an issue, write down something about that. Maybe you'll eat half of your meal today?" Miss Maroon offered. "Or maybe you'll stop thinking about the person that had you admitted for one hour."

My eyes dropped to my notebook. A pen had been placed beside it, though I had no idea how it ended up there. Laces and Varla had already started writing, so I opened my notebook and tried to follow suit as best I could.

"No one can look at your journal, so write whatever you want. As long as you get something down on paper, we'll consider that a victory." Miss Maroon insisted.

I didn't have any goals ready, so I wrote whatever came to mind and swore I would be better prepared for the next day.

Journal Entry #1

I was heavily medicated and almost drowned in a stack of pancakes.
Hannibal Sketcher rescued me.
I met a girl named Varla, who seems pretty nice.
(She needs to gain a few pounds)
Wondering how my mom is doing.
GOALS: Try not to think of new and exciting ways to kill Joe.

Good job. I smiled back at my handiwork and glanced at Laces—who was now on his second freakin' page. "Brown-noser," I whispered under my breath.

Laces bared his teeth, but didn't look up at me. "As flattering as that compliment is, I can't take credit for someone else's work."

"Hmm?"

His eyes flashed to mine. "I'm writing song lyrics." And when my forehead creased in confusion he gave me a look, "*Snuff* by Slipknot."

My mouth popped open. "Ohhh."

He did a double take of me, his eyes filling with humor as I flushed. "You didn't actually write down your feelings, did you?"

"No."

Sort of…

NINE

Gambrielle
———————————

THE ONE PART of the first day that I had been dreading—aside from being stuck around Laces & Co—was meeting with my therapist, Dr. Young. My mother had been to therapy over the years and spoken about the experience during her drunken spells; they always wanted to get down to the root of the problem by talking about your feelings, and picking off old wounds that were best left as scars.

Dr. Young was no different.

From the moment I walked into his office, closed the door, and took my seat in the vacant chair on the other side of his desk, I knew I was in for an hour of hell. His kind smiles, cool demeanor, and occasional chuckle did very little to cut the tension in the room.

"Where would you like to start, Gambrielle?" Dr. Young asked, rocking back and forth in his black leather seat. There was an open folder on his desk, post-it's at the ready, and a pen glued to his forefinger. He was prepared to get down to the business of examining my traumatized psyche. "Your file mentioned that you have a sister, Eliza-beth…why don't we talk about her?"

At the sound of her name my shoulders tensed and my heart sped up like a jack-hammer on steroids. I wanted to indulge in her existence, to tell him everything that she was and would never be. How she loved traveling, animals, sad chick flicks, and life. Chewing on my lower lip, I shook my head. "There's not really much to say." I finally said. "She's gone."

And she was never coming back.

Joe had seen to that.

Dr. Young stopped rocking in his chair. "You had a lot to say about her in court." He reminded me, and tears filled the corners of my eyes as he glanced back at my case file. "Elizabeth wanted to be a nurse?" He tapped the paper, "You mentioned that she often cleaned you up after Joe had one of his episodes."

"I was referring to how she used to be, before Joe…" Before, Elizabeth could walk, talk, and do anything her heart desired. Now she was six feet under.

Dr. Young slid his finger down the first page of my file, looking for anything of value to push the conversation forward. He stopped midway to the bottom of the page, his serious gaze flashing to me. "You told Judge Wexler that you had dreams about Joe and his abusive behavior. Would you care to elaborate on that?" His voice was polite, the way a therapist should behave. But I couldn't let my guard down. Since the trial everything I said had been used against me and I didn't want to add anything to the outstanding list of things that Joe could benefit from.

Joe was the District Attorney. He had power, money, connections—everything he needed to take me down and make my stay at Hawthorne a permanent situation. As much as I wanted my own peace-of-mind, I craved justice more. "No, I don't…I don't remember much about anything." I stammered, forcing out the lies.

"I'm here for you, Gambrielle. You understand that, right? I already know everything that happened."

"Then why do you need me to say it, hmm?" My words were clipped, my tone full of annoyance. "I am doing my best to make it out of this in one piece. Not the whole piece, maybe tattered fragments, but still something worth salvaging. Can't you see that?!" It was the only way I knew how to beg for pity and understanding.

Unfortunately, I didn't sell myself well enough. Because instead of patting me on the back and telling me *we'll try again some other time*, or *you've had a hard day, Gambrielle*, Dr. Young went straight for the jugular. Emotions be damned.

"What about Jaguar?" Dr. Young asked, and my body instantly froze. *Oh God.* Anyone but *him*. No! Dr. Young's finger skimmed down my chart, stopping at what I could only assume was Jag's *E! True Hollywood Story*. Curiosity entered his eyes and he raised a light brow. Something had caught his attention.

I bit my lower lip as I waited for him to continue his interrogation. I knew Jag was in the report. How could he not be? I had seen him almost every day for two years straight. He was one of the first people the police went to for a character witness. "What does Jag have to do with anything?" Like me, he had already dealt with enough from Joe and deserved to be left out of this.

Dr. Young nodded. "He was Elizabeth's boyfriend, right?"

"I-don't-want-to-talk-about-Jag." I said in a rush. "We can talk about my mom, if you want, or…I don't know, my grandmother! She witnessed a lot too!" I was now leaning forward, elbows on his desk, trying desperately to shift the topic elsewhere. I didn't want to tell him anything, but he had touched upon a super sensitive spot in my soul that I wanted to lay to rest. Jag deserved that much. "Okay, how about this: I'll tell you about the first time I had to go to the hospital. Every-little-bit-of-it. Nothing left out. That work?" Bargaining wasn't my best quality, but he seemed like a man who appreciated a little give and take. Plus, my first trip to the hospital because of Joe's actions wasn't as traumatic as everyone probably thought. I'd been hit with a belt as punishment for not finishing a can of soda. Joe had called it wasteful, and in the midst of his rage hit my lip with the metal belt buckle. The four stitches across my eyebrow had been painful, but it was nothing compared to the future damage he would inflict.

Yes, I'll let him have the first visit. Joe could win this one. There was medical documentation to back-up my claim, anyway. I nodded at my thoughts and blew out a deep breath, preparing myself, mentally, to make the treacherous trip back down memory lane. "I wore a yellow parka that day. It had rained the night before..."

A sad smile splayed across Dr. Young's lips. Before I had a chance to continue, he flipped to the second page of my chart and said, "Do you want to go home? Or do you want to stay in here forever?" He leaned forward to meet me halfway and added, "Forever in a place like this is a long time, Gambrielle. I've treated patients that have been housed in facilities just like this one for over twenty years. One or two years?" He made a face. "That's not so bad. Twenty years? That's a third of your life." His sympathetic eyes pierced into mine. "Are you going to stay here and give up? Or are you going to fight with me?"

I opened my mouth to speak but couldn't find the words to justify my defense. No, I didn't want to stay at Hawthorne forever. I wanted to get out, go to college, grow old, maybe have a few kids. I'd never been the most atten-tive to my cousins, Xander and Zavier, whenever they came to visit during the holidays, but I was working toward it. I'd also envisioned a teaching career in literature and spending the majority of my days reciting old works from some of history's greatest writers. The point was: I had made goals, and I knew how to work toward them to make them a reality. And as soon as justice was served to Joe on a platter, I would pick myself back up and forge ahead as best I could. That was all anyone could do in my predicament, right?

"I want to go home." I softly admitted, leaning back in my seat. "But I don't have a home to go back to."

Dr. Young settled his elbows on his desk and propped his palms under his chin. "That's a scary thought." he agreed. "Would it make you feel better to know most of the patients here are in the same boat?"

No, it didn't. All it did was make me feel worse.

"I can get you home. It may not be the home you are used to, and at times it might get lonely but," Dr. Young paused for effect, "you'll have your freedom."

I nodded.

"I'm not here for your family, I'm here for you. "

I was stubborn, and rightfully so after everything I had endured over the last six months, which Dr. Young picked up on right away. When twenty minutes passed and we hadn't made any progress, he reached into his desk and retrieved an unopened pack of shiny, yellow stars. *What's this*? It seemed stupid, the power those stars held over me; instantly, my body sat at attention and my eyes focused on the five points.

"Two stars. That's what I'm offering, Gambrielle." he said. "You tell me about Jaguar, *not Elizabeth*, but Jaguar."

Two stars?

Two days.

For the price of one?

I bit my lip as Dr. Young waved the pack in front of me

as though it were a million dollars. "Two stars. Going once, going twice—"

"—Joe hated him." I blurted out. *Crap, here we go.* Clasping my hands together in my lap, I squeezed my eyes shut and blew out a deep breath. "He, um… Jag, was a police officer."

Dr. Young ceased his movements but continued to hold the stars up like a torch signifying freedom. "What do you mean by *Joe hated him*? Why?"

I pursed my lips together. "Because Jag wielded more power than he did."

"More control, you mean?" Dr. Young assumed.

"No." I wagged my head. "It was more than that."

"Oh?"

"Joe *wanted* to be the law. Jag *was*—well, *is*—the law." *Two stars.* I had to keep reminding myself of that even as Dr. Young pulled out a legal pad and began scribbling things down. Two stars, eight days left, if I could manage to get through the next ten minutes.

"How old is Jaguar?"

It seemed a basic enough question. "Twenty-three, I think."

Dr. Young nodded but didn't stop jotting down the information. "And how old was your sister?"

"Eighteen."

"That's a pretty big age gap." Dr. Young noted. He peeked over his legal pad and raised a questioning brow. "Did Joe take issue with that?"

I shook my head. "Age was never the issue. Jag wanted to marry her and show her the world." A smile tugged at my lips as a memory of Jag in his policeman uniform flipping pancakes entered my frontal lobe. I don't know what it was about him that warmed my soul; perhaps the way he treated her, as though she were a precious mirage that could vanish at any moment if his brain veered too far away. Anything she wanted, all she had to do was ask—he was that devoted and consumed by her.

"Jag didn't take any of his crap." I finally said, looking back at Dr. Young. "He stood up to him. He was her shield."

Dr. Young tilted his head back and let out a sympathetic, "ahhh."

"Jag used to pick us up every morning in his police cruiser and take us to school. We always had to stay ducked down in the backseat because he wasn't allowed to let anyone ride with him…but Jag being Jag, he was determined to give her the whole high school boyfriend experience."

"And did he?" Dr. Young pressed on.

My brows knitted. "I think so." My eyes fell to the white knuckles suffocating in my lap. "She always wrote about him in her diary and would sometimes show me a few pages…" My words drifted off as the revelation slammed into me like a ton of bricks.

Diary…

Would there be anything in her diary, besides Jag? I'd never thought to ask, nor had she ever offered up the information. What if she had written something important that the investigators missed?

Things were quiet for the next few minutes as Dr. Young jotted down the remainder of his notes. I didn't care. I was too preoccupied with thoughts of what could be in between the pages of the small black book. Had Elizabeth written about the abuse she had endured at the hands of Joe? Had Joe tried to kill her before six months ago? He'd wanted to silence her and was eventually successful in his quest. But did she leave a trail for me to pick up on and follow?

Please God…

I needed that diary.

"Our time is up. Same time on Thursday?" Dr. Young said, breaking the silence.

I tore my eyes away from the window I'd been looking at. "My stars?"

"I'll put them on the hp board before I go home."

"Thank you."

I rose from my seat and damn near tripped when I heard, "Where do you think the diary is?"

Holy mother of… "Excuse me?"

"You want the diary."

"I didn't say that."

"You didn't have to. It's written all over your face." Dr. Young smirked. "There must be something vital in it."

I casually shrugged. "Don't know. Elizabeth was a very private person."

Dr. Young held up three fingers. "Three stars, Gambrielle."

I couldn't hide the shock that registered in my expression. The man knew how to bargain, that was for sure.

"Answer my question and I'll go stick the stars up right now." Dr. Young said, leaning back in his seat. He slowly rocked back and forth, smiling back at me, but not in a malicious way. Not like Joe would've. His smile was warm, purposeful, like he truly wanted what was best for me.

Assuming I had nothing to lose, I rubbed my forehead and said, "It's probably hidden somewhere in her room, or maybe the garage out back." When Dr. Young didn't move to write the information down, I gestured toward his legal pad. "Aren't you supposed to be writing this down?"

"What for?" He gave a subtle wink and relief filled my chest. Jerking his chin to the door he said, "Have a good day, Gambrielle."

"You too, Dr. Young." I was confused and relieved by his kindness but didn't question it as I moved for the door. I didn't want to push my luck.

Laces was staked out directly across from Dr. Young's door—back leaned against the wall, one leg nonchalantly crossed over the other, looking like a bad boy coming to collect in his black scrubs. He had his sketchpad in one hand, a pencil in the other, and seemed to be going to town with his latest conquest. Without looking up, he asked. "And how was therapy?"

I shoved my hands in my black scrub pockets. "Not that it's any of your business, but it went fine."

"How many stars did you make out with?" he asked. Dusting some charcoal residue off of his sketch, he peeked up with a sexy smirk. "Tell me you at least got five."

"Three." Before he could give me a lecture on whatever I had done wrong, which seemed to be his style, I started down the hallway back toward my room. Hearing his footsteps following behind I rolled my eyes and picked up a little speed, which he matched effortlessly. "Don't you have something else to do?"

"I already fucked Nurse Kline, so my schedule is wide open," he released a deep breath and added, "and so is hers." I could hear him smiling as the statement fell through his lips. Coming to a dead halt, I swirled around to face him, eyes as wide as the sky, my mouth practically hitting the floor. Why I expected anything different from him, I had no idea. Men like him were hardwired to be assholes, it was engrained in their DNA or something. And shamefully, I found myself feeling the same disappointment as I had felt earlier. Amused by my puzzled expression, he put his pencil in his mouth and turned his latest masterpiece around, wiggling his eyebrows as his muffled voice said, "What do you think?"

The "masterpiece" was Nurse Kline sprawled out on a bed—probably his—naked, with her arms bound, mouth duct taped, and a shiny blade ripping through her chest. Shockingly, I wasn't as disturbed by this sketch as much as my own. Everything was sketched to perfection—her eyes, mouth, and even the heart studs she wore. In another life he could've given Picasso a run for his money.

"Isn't sleeping with Nurse Kline breaking the rules?" I asked, looking up at him.

Laces grinned back at me. "Some break rules, I break beds. We all have our talents."

"You're disgusting!"

Laces let out a dreamy sigh, "And yet you STILL fainted!"

My lips popped open. *Oh no he didn't…*

Without thinking, I reached forward and gave him a hard shove, gawking when his toned body didn't move an inch. He was like a statue, every inch sculpted to resemble that of a God. Cocking his head to the side he looked at me with a delightful sinners gaze, his head to the side and gazed at me with his blue inscrutable eyes.

All I could do was stand there—eyes narrowed; lips pressed—as he reveled in his victory. I had no retort for his allegations, not a single witty comeback. He was grinning ear-to-ear as I turned and made a beeline for my room. The thought of him holding the fainting spell against me for the rest of our days was almost unbearable.

Laces, 3. Me, 0.

TEN

Laces

THE WAY GAMBRIELLE looked at me when I told her about Nurse Kline, the pity and revulsion swimming around in her eyes—fuck. It was like watching an episode of Jerry Springer, and not just any episode, but a real cringe-worthy one; the kind that made you put down the chips and beer and start taking serious notes after the first chair was thrown.

Fuck me.

It took less than ten seconds—a turn from Gambrielle, and a swift exit left—for me to become that bastard who had just told his soul mate that he enjoyed chicken wings and fuckin' her morbidly obese sister.

Or at least that was how it felt…

I sucked in a sharp breath between my teeth and clenched my fists. Nurse Kline had not been a part of the plan—she hadn't even made it to the blueprint—but do you know what had? Survival. And behind the sterile white walls of Hawthorne a war raged on, and war was not without its casualties. Nurse Kline's body was a necessary

84

casualty to keep me marching day-in-and-day-out through the bloody trenches. I needed her.

And it was best Gambrielle knew that up front, just in case she got a wild hair up her ass and thought I was boyfriend material. *No baby, uh-uh…*

"Just so you know: I hurt for you." Peering over my shoulder, I smirked at the sight of Reyes leaned against the wall, chewing on an apple. "Innocent, naïve, vulnerable—I get it. She's like anime porn for nerds."

"So why aren't you trying to fuck her?"

Shooting me a stern look, Reyes' kicked off of the wall and took his place beside me. "Because women like her don't belong in our orbit. She belongs in some farmhouse with blue gingham curtains or something," he paused, appearing to be in deep thought, "with the white picket fence, devoted husband, and kids that look like Gerber babies. You and I are entitled to three things." He held up three fingers and began ticking them off, "1) a drug problem, 2) four ex-wives bleeding our bank accounts dry, and 3) a sultry mistress in the Hamptons."

I raised a brow. "What if she gives me the drug problem?"

Reyes's head fell back. He groaned. "Jesus, Laces—"

"If she gives me the drug problem, I am entitled to her, four ex-wives, and the mistress." I pointed out, grinning wide. I didn't believe for a second that Gambrielle would be the cause of my hypothetical drug problem, but it was worth saying just to see the aggravation creep across Reyes' face. He was so serious all of the time and didn't know when to let loose. Slapping my hand across his back, I said, "Relax. Stray isn't even on my radar. She's just something to play with." The fact that she was something new went without saying.

"I know you." Reyes said, running his hands through

his hair. He gripped the ends and shot me a worried look, "Please, for the love of God, keep it in your pants."

Hey, I'm praying for that too man, I wanted to say, but settled for a firm nod. There was no point in getting Reyes worked up over something that hadn't even happened yet —and with the seed I'd just planted, probably wouldn't anytime soon.

THE DAYS FOLLOWING my Nurse Kline confession were peculiar to say the least. It was the first time I'd ever blurted out that type of information to a stranger, and if I'm being honest with myself, it had me a little concerned. I wasn't a *blurter*. No, I was the bastard shooting the go-fuck-yourself bullets at close range in the brain, and on occasion, the comedic relief. But a blurter?

I could've said anything else to drive Gambrielle away —like having a three inch cock or something,

I feel like it is imperative to mention, I didn't have a three inch cock, but I knew that no sane woman would find the measurements remotely appealing, *so…*

The first day following the confession was difficult. Every time Gambrielle looked at me, I could feel the displeasure radiating from her body like a visceral shock-wave. Her eyes burned holes through mine, her sharp nails tapped away at her desk like a knife cutting through a fresh piece of meat. Normally women—even those who knew I was a player and a grade-A douchebag—threw themselves at me. But not Gambrielle. She had gotten the hint and took my confession as gospel.

"I know we're in a psych ward, but since we're going to be friends, I feel the need to give you the lowdown on the men of this floor. It'll save you a lot of time, honey, trust me." Varla quipped to Gambrielle during lunch one afternoon . Her bright blue hair was neatly tucked behind her ears, showcasing the clown make-up she'd become notorious for. Today she'd slapped on bright shades of pink and purple. I wanted to take my napkin, lean across the table, and take a slow swipe across her small face to make a point. Stabbing her fork into a small piece of watermelon, Varla turned to Gambrielle and whispered, "The only man worth having is Thorne."

Excuse—the-fuck-outta—me?

My fork fell to my plate with a clatter, and my lips parted slightly. I shouldn't have been pissed off at Varla's forwardness, but I was. *What the fuck, Varla?!* Even if I wasn't worth someone's time or effort, she should've upheld her loyalty and presented me as a black knight, a prince, or whatever bullshit the women fantasized over these days.

Clasping my hands together under my chin, I propped my elbows on the table and took a quick look at Reyes, who was seated on the other side of Varla. He didn't look too pleased either, but continued to chow down on his spaghetti while shooting Varla his best fuck-me-eyes every chance he could. *What a trooper...*

And Thorne? He had his nose buried in a crossword puzzle, oblivious to everything going on around him.

Varla jerked her head to the left, where Reyes was seated. "He has commitment issues." Her voice was barely audible.

Gambrielle smiled at her burger. "Too afraid to commit?" she said with a chuckle.

"No, he gets too committed." Varla threw her head back, as did Gambrielle, and they both laughed like hyenas. And yeah, a snicker or two slipped through my own mouth because I'll admit that shit was funny.

But then Varla's eyes flickered to me, "Laces is the direct opposite. He doesn't believe in commitment—and even if he did, his sketchbook wouldn't allow it."

My eyes briefly widened so as not to draw attention to myself. I wasn't one to get embarrassed, but even I could feel the heat building up in my cheeks as Gambrielle slapped a hand over her mouth and snorted. Yep, I was going to kill Varla and donate her make-up supply to the nearest damn clown college!

Someone snorted. *Reyes*. With one kick to his shin I shut that shit down real quick. He hissed through his teeth and I sliced a hand across my throat. *Shut-up asshole!*

"Not that I can blame Laces, though." Varla whispered in a hush-hush voice seconds later. "His girlfriend, Lexi—"

She didn't even have her full name out and already the red alarms were going off in my head. "Enough, Varla!" I snapped, shoving my chair back. I rose to my feet, along with Reyes. Thorne had just found Lemons in his crossword puzzle and wasn't abandoning it for anyone.

"Oh my God—I'm so sorry Laces!" Varla quickly jumped to her feet, "I got carried away."

I held up my palm. "Thorne!" I snapped. The entire cafeteria was now staring at our table, including Lunch-Lady Halpert. But I didn't give a damn. I kicked Thorne's chair and his eyes shot to me. "Let's go!"

"I just found Minnesota." Thorne muttered.

"Find your balls and get up." Reyes quipped.

Gambrielle's eyes widened as Thorne slammed his puzzle book shut and shoved his seat back with a loud screech. Rising to his feet he saluted Varla, then Gambrielle, before stomping away with me and Reyes.

The second day of my "Gambrielle Embargo", was equally as difficult. I had yet to make peace with Varla speaking of Lexi and was on edge. Sometimes, not often, I would speak of Lexi in therapy, but never in public. She was a part of my past life, a life that broke me, and hearing Varla dangle her name out there so freely hit a serious nerve in my black soul.

So I did what any man in my position would do.

"I need alcohol. Vodka, specifically. Lots of vodka." I murmured to Nurse Kline before recreational therapy. She was busy filling out a release form and simply nodded from behind the nurses' station. "Is that a yes?"

"No." She hummed. Her blonde hair was pulled back into a tight bun with little wispy strands hanging every which way. It suited her. Peeking up from the form, she tilted her head to the left and raised a perfectly groomed brow, "What do I get in return?"

I smirked. "Me."

"I already have you." She cooed.

I leaned against the counter and lowered my voice, "ANAL." I had performed anal a few times in my life and the women loved it. It was usually reserved for special moments, like after getting a blow job for a solid hour straight. But this one time I was willing to make the sacrifice in exchange for getting shit-faced. *Tit for tat.*

Nurse Kline hummed her approval in a low groan. "As tempting as that is, I'm afraid you would tear me in two." she said, pouting at me. "And Ken already takes care of that, so I'm going to have to pass. What else do you have to offer?"

Fuck.

Ken was her husband. At the start of our arrangement, he was going through a mid-life crisis, so things were pretty easy for us. She would suck me off, we'd have sex in the boiler room, and I would go down on her out of pity. The way I saw it a window had opened and opportunity was calling my name. That opportunity had served me well, at least until recently when Ken decided to get back in bed and ride his horse.

I sighed. "What do you need?"

Nurse Kline's lips curved into a sadistic smile, one I knew all too well. Rising from her seat, she leaned over the counter until our faces were an inch apart. Her wintergreen tinged breath slammed into my lungs as her mischievous eyes held mine. "You're friends with Evans, correct?"

I pulled back a little and studied her face. "Hmm?"

"*Evans*." She mouthed, and leaned toward my ear and whispered, "The girl in the room across from you. Gambrielle Evans."

The muscles in my back instantly went stiff. "What about her?" And what about my Vodka? I needed it, now!

With a sly grin, Nurse Kline fell back into her seat and began digging through a filing cabinet. A couple of patients strolled by, but didn't bother stopping. Finding a manila folder buried in the back, Nurse Kline said, "I'll be right back" and walked to Dr. Folton's office to make a copy. She returned a few minutes later with a smug look on her face and slid the new copy across the counter. I didn't look down.

"Aren't you the least bit curious about what I want?" she asked coquettishly, batting her long lashes.

"I'm sure you're going to tell me." *You always do*, I thought wryly.

She flexed two fingers and I followed her to the janitor's room ten feet away. It was humid in there, uncomfortably so, but I settled on an old table and folded my arms, waiting to hear her out.

"You know she is DA Evans' stepdaughter?"

I shrugged. And what did this have to do with my alcohol?

"He has agreed to fund a fourth floor for Hawthorne,

but he won't write the check until Evans has been transferred to Floor C."

Floor C. *The Suicide Floor*. Everyone up there had given up on life and/or wanted to die. Most wore straitjackets and ate via feeding tubes. I'd never been up there, but I'd heard a few stories in passing.

"I want you to drive her crazy, do you understand?" Nurse Kline said. Her eyes surveyed my entire body from top to bottom. "I need you to get her put on Floor C. You do that and I'll give you whatever you want."

"But I need alcohol NOW." I pointed out. "Getting her transferred to another floor could take months."

"I'll supply you with some vodka upfront." she said.

I blinked. If it had been anyone else I wouldn't have thought twice, and I think Nurse Kline knew it too. Flopping down in a dusty seat nearby, she smiled up at me. "I give you full permission to fuck her and do whatever you need to do in order to secure the deal." She added, and yet I still didn't leap. What was wrong with my dark soul? Turning away, I closed my eyes and took a deep breath. I'd done a lot of fucked-up things in my life, but I'd never driven anyone crazy just to do it. In the bedroom, yes, but in an asylum? Even I wasn't that fucked-up.

When I didn't immediately leap at Nurse Kline's offer she cleared her throat and said, "If you don't want to do it I could always ask Reyes or Thorne."

"I didn't say no."

"You didn't say yes, either though." Nurse Kline innocently said. Rising to her feet, she seductively cornered me alongside the boiler and whispered into my ear, all breathy, "You're supposed to be my crazy boy, hmm? Thorne's my devil, the one always telling me no. Not you."

I squeezed my eyes shut and pursed my lips. Shit.

"Don't make me bring a fourth guy into the mix."

Nurse Kline warned. "You, Reyes, and Thorne have it easy. You guys fuck me whenever you need something, and in return I give you orgasms and whatever your heart's desire."

Shit…shit, shit fuck!

"I don't…know if I can." I slowly said, cracking my eyes. The corners of her lips quirked up. "She hates me." She needed to know upfront the battle I would be facing with that one. Gambrielle and I couldn't say much without stirring up an argument, and as confident as I was about my ability to seduce a woman and drive her crazy, even I questioned my level of expertise where Gambrielle was involved.

"I hated you when I first met you and look at us now." Nurse Kline whispered, smiling up at me. "Make her fall in love with you and rip her heart out."

"I have a tight schedule." I mused.

"According to her chart she is a virgin." Nurse Kline went on, just packing in on and on. "Don't you have a thing for virgins? Or is that Reyes?"

I sighed. "How long?"

She pressed her cheek to my chest. "So is that a yes?"

Was it?

"How long?" I repeated.

"Three months, max."

"Holy shit—"

"—It'll fly by so quick." Nurse Kline assured me.

Bullshit.

B-U-L-L-S-H-I-T.

Pushing her off of me I shook my head. "I don't know what love is—you need to go to Reyes." It killed me to pass the buck along, but I didn't want to fail her. She was my survival at Hawthorne. I needed to keep her happy, and failure wouldn't do me any favors in that department.

"No." she said from behind as I reached for the door. Her words caught me off guard and I froze midway. "I want you to do it. Reyes would take it too personally," she paused, "and Thorne would drive himself crazy in the process. You're the only one I can count on to keep it purely professional."

ELEVEN

Gambrielle
_____

I HAD BEEN at Hawthorne for less than a week when the rumors started. Varla said it came with the territory, that everyone at Hawthorne had their day to endure their walk of shame. "It's a rite of passage." She had explained during lunch. "Just keep your head down and pay no attention to what they say."

"I can't believe she lied."

"I can. Look at her! Just another pissed-off southern belle who didn't get what she wanted."

"No."

"Uh-yesss. I did my research yesterday during rec therapy. The big three—National Enquirer, The Sun, The Times—all have eyewitness accounts that say Evans lost it after her step-daddy wouldn't pay for a super slutty dress."

Oh now that is not true!

I would never.

The only time I had ever gotten upset about anything materialistic was at junior prom; the dress—a tight, sparkly number—had ripped going down the spiral staircase of our five bedroom estate. I had become upset, but in the end held it together and fixed the situation with safety pins.

Pursing my lips, I slumped down in my desk and glared at the gossip patrol in front of me. Both were hunched over their desks, whispering to the other patients in front of them. It was like watching a cyclone come together, every student was sucked in.

Miss Maroon was scribbling a few sentences on the blackboard and every few seconds would glance over her shoulder to see the commotion. The chitchat didn't stop, even after she'd threatened to remove day points, so she gave up and ignored them.

Just like high school…

"Don't just sit there." I heard Laces whisper. He was seated on the right side of me, elbow propped on the desk, his black unruly hair tucked back with his hand. This was the first time he had spoken to me in three days so I was a bit unprepared for his bluntness.

"I'm sorry, are you talking to me?" I asked in a prissy tone.

His bright blue eyes were glued to the blackboard. "Don't be a pussy, stray."

I scoffed. "I'm not a—"I lowered my voice, flushing, "*PUSSYYY!!* It's called picking your battles."

"Sounds like surrendering to me." Laces murmured through the corner of his tempting lips. It amazed me that even dressed in nothing more than a black hoodie and scrub garb he still managed to pull off looking like a Greek God, and secretly I hated him for it…

"I wouldn't expect someone like *you* to understand my actions." I said, turning my attention back to Miss Maroon. She was in the middle of an animated tale involving herself, drugs, and a rollercoaster. Very heavy stuff apparently.

"What the hell is that supposed to mean?" Laces' voice, normally low and raw, was deeper now. More serious.

My brows shot up. Until that moment I didn't know he possessed a serious bone in his body. I played it cool, pretending to jot down some notes as the first of several kicks came to the leg of my chair. I'd hit a nerve, clearly, and made a mental note of it for future occasions. "What does that mean?" Laces repeated; another kick. "I can keep doing this all day…"

"What is your real name?" I asked, attempting to change the subject. There wasn't enough time to go neck deep into the conversation he was demanding us to have.

"None of your damn business," Laces said, "and what did you mean by someone like *you*?"

A sweet smile spread across my lips. "Sorry, my attorney told me to never give out any information for free. Come back with an adequate form of payment and we'll talk."

Flipping a curly, brown strand over my shoulder, I let out a happy sigh and flipped to the next page of my journal. Laces' sexual endeavors—COUGHS, his confession of bedding Nurse Kline—would make for an interesting entry.

I could feel his harsh gaze on me; feel the tapping of his foot against my chair for the next ten minutes. Neither of us spoke or acknowledged each other's presence. Typical. I didn't know how to give an inch and he always wanted a mile.

Toward the end of group therapy the kicking abruptly stopped and I felt him lean toward me. His musky scent was lethal, practically intoxicating as he whispered, "Alright, I'll tell you my real name. But I want to know what you meant."

I kept my eyes zeroed in on my journal. "You first."

A chuckle rumbled through his chest. "Hell no."

"I can't trust you to come through with your end of the deal." I said demurely. Through the corner of my eye I could see his lips twitching. "What's so funny?"

He nodded at me. "You."

"What about me?"

"Your paranoia—it's cute."

Cuteeee. Flushing, I turned away.

"Yes, cute. It's a compliment, a term of endearment?"

"I know what it is." Putting my pencil down, I closed my notebook and propped my elbows on the desk. I was the picture perfect image of a secretary scorned, minus the hideous black scrubs. "You want to know what I meant by someone like *you*? Fine. You don't see people for who they are, but rather what they can give you. People are objects to you, chess pieces for you to play with." I gestured towards the gossip brigade a few rows forward, "At any time you could've stopped them from running their mouths about me, but you didn't because it wouldn't benefit you. And calling me cute right now? It's nothing more than a desperate ploy to get what you want," I took a deep breath and slowly exhaled, "cute might work on the blonde bimbos you wait in line with for nightly meds, but not on me. I don't care one iota about your bad boy demeanor and indifference toward life."

His lips broke into a million dollar smile that damn near knocked the breath right out of me. "You've been checking up on me."

"Hardly."

"Then how would you know who I associate with during my off time?"

I held up my palm. "Oh please. It's practically impossible not to notice your little fangirls squealing."

"Lincoln Caster."

"Hum?"

"You wanted to know what my real name was. It's Lincoln Caster." His eyes dropped to my lips and—I don't know why but the Gods decided to forsake me then and there. There was a desire in his eyes, so possessive and fierce, like he wanted to make a four course meal out of me in group therapy. He reached forward and tucked a loose strand behind my ear; his finger brushed across my skin, sending a jolt of electricity coursing through my body. "I'm going to say this because I don't want there to be any gray areas between us."

Oh?

I was under his spell and sat a little taller. "Yes?"

"I don't want anything from you but friendship." He gestured between us, "We can keep this charade up all day, every day, or we can put away our swords and try to make the best of this hellhole."

I was floored. "That's the most adult thing I've heard come out of your mouth." It really was.

Miss Maroon dismissed us shortly thereafter, and Laces jumped to his feet, bowing like an 1800's servant. He offered his hand, "Milady."

My lips twitched and as much as I didn't want to, I smiled. "Why thank you, kind sir." I said, accepting his gallant gesture. The same electric current attacked my skin as he helped me to my feet.

"See, now was that so hard?" Laces asked once I was standing in front of him.

Somewhat embarrassed, it took everything in me to mumble a pathetic "no", and I could tell by the amusement swirling around in his blue orbs that he knew it too. Why the sudden change? Had my honesty gotten to him? Had he woken up and decided I was worthy of his friendship? *Or maybe worthy of his bed?* Maybe this was his way of trying to get in my cotton panties.

I shook the thoughts off and continued to smile as I followed him out of group therapy and into the main hallway.

We were in a psych ward, and aside from Varla, I had no one. I wasn't exactly in a position to pass-up kindness, even if that kindness came from Laces. Out in the pristine hallway he gestured for me to follow him to a group of patients that had formed near his room. The slut brigade.

"I know you're a country girl, stray, and you want to be civil, but in here that shit won't fly. You'll get pushed over." he said over his shoulder. The group of five or so girls parted like the Red Sea as we got closer. I noticed the two girls that had been gossiping standing in the far back, closest to Laces door. Stopping in front of the group Laces clasped his hands behind his back and said, "Which of you bitches is talking shit?"

There was no introduction.

No "hi, how are you doing?"

Nothing.

His words begged for anyone to test him.

I'd stopped a foot behind and whispered, "I wasn't asking you to help me. I was using it as an example. You don't have to do this."

"Oh, but I do." Laces said, grinning back at me. He turned to face his slut brigade. None of them were owning up to anything. They all looked like scared rats ready to flee a sinking ship. "SHE IS MINE." And it was the way he said it, all cryptic, that left me and everyone else floored. He pointed a tan finger in my direction, "You don't touch what's mine; you don't speak about what's mine. Because if you do I'll make my sketches a reality and gut you in your sleep."

"Hey!" I whispered with a hiss. His narrow eyes peeked over his shoulder. "I'm not yours! And don't joke like that. We're in a psych ward, remember? They could report us."

Laces licked his thick lips in that way that bad boys do and chuckled. "What makes you think I was joking?"

My stomach dropped. "Huh? What if this gets around to your um—Nurse Kline! I can't afford to lose any points." *Or my life…* I wasn't sure how involved they were, but I wasn't willing to chance it because he wanted to be some badass.

"Don't worry about it. Let me take care of it." He turned back to the girls. All of their eyes were wide, their faces ghostly pale. One of the girls had tightly crossed her legs and I couldn't help but wonder if her bodily functions down below had failed her somehow. "This is your only warning. Understand? Next time I'll be mailing body parts to your mother."

Hannibal Sketcher….

JOURNAL ENTRY #4

If anyone's body parts go missing I had nothing to do with it, LINCOLN CASTER is the culprit. Varla and I are becoming fast friends. I'm not really big on make-up, but it's fun to watch her create different designs. We share a love for country music/Taylor Swift. She gave me some tic-tacs and I've been taking them during morning meds. It's pretty easy to get away with. When a nurse sees something white in your mouth they automatically assume its medication and don't look into it.

**My mother hasn't tried to get in touch with me.
No letters or phone calls.
I did receive a get well card from my attorney,
Malcolm, along with an unpaid bill of $58,488
dollars...I don't know how I'm going to come up
with that money. During lunch Laces suggested
setting up shop on the corner, but later in the
commons room, when we were alone, he said he
would see what he could do.
Star count: 6.
4 more stars and I get a weekend pass to go home!**

"YOU'RE NOT to see him again, cunt." Joe's words spit into Elizabeth's face. "And where do you think you're going dressed like that? Not out of this house."

I'd hidden in the closet of her bedroom. There was a small crack from where the door hadn't shut completely which allowed me to see what was going on. Elizabeth was sitting at the edge of her bed, legs crossed, with a black miniskirt barely covering her upper thighs. I'd warned her to leave before Joe got home, but she adamantly refused. She wanted to look her best for Jaguar. "You can't keep me from seeing him." she said, sounding unmoved.

Joe bent over in front of her, his beer belly hanging over his belt like a second skin. "You'll do whatever I tell you! I pay the bills around here!"

"Then I'll move in with Jaguar."

This angered Joe even more. He grabbed her cell phone from the bed and proudly held it up for her to see. "Good luck getting ahold of him. You'll get your phone back when you start treating me with some damn respect."

Unlike me, Elizabeth knew no boundaries when it came to Joe. Everything he said went into one ear and out the other. Seeing Joe tuck her phone into his back pocket, she shrugged. "He'll stop by when I don't answer." she said, smiling up at him. "And if you don't let him in he'll go over your head and claim to be doing a welfare check."

Joe was still posturing in front of her like an ape. "Your cop better stay in his fuckin' lane, do you hear me?" he shouted. His face was blood red and sweat had begun to accumulate on his brows. Without warning, he smacked her across the face and she cried out. He rose to his feet, muttering the same words over and over as he headed for the door, "you're not to see him ever again!"

Elizabeth covered her red cheek with her hand and glared up at him. He was three times her size, but she held her own. Reaching under her bed she pulled out her softball bat and got into position. "You piece of shit."

Joe stopped at the doorway. His harsh breathing sent fear ricocheting throughout my entire body as he turned to face her. I'd never seen him so upset.

The corner of Elizabeth's lips tugged up. "I'm not weak like my mother, Joe. And if you think I am, come on over here and let's see how weak I can be." She snarled.

He took a step forward and she tightened her grip on the bat. For a minute I thought there was going to be serious bloodshed all over her pastel colored room.

"I'm going to beat your ass." Joe said, as though it were everyday conversation. He stopped a foot away from her and taunted, "It's you or Gambrielle. Someone's going to pay for my troubles…"

Elizabeth didn't bow. "You touch me or Gam again, and I'll let Jaguar have you." She threatened.

"You can't hide behind that boyfriend forever. One day you'll be alone and…"

Feeling a warm finger tracing over the branding on my wrist, I cracked my eyes. My scrubs were soaked in sweat and I could hear my heart pounding through my ears. It was late, far past the time for lights out, but I could still make out his lean silhouette as he released my wrist and moved toward the door.

"Laces." I whispered.

He was halfway to the door and stilled. "Hmm?"

"I didn't do it to myself if that's what you're thinking." I said, referring to the branding.

He said nothing.

I didn't bother offering up an explanation, nor did I ask the why's and how's of how he was there to begin with. I couldn't believe it, but his presence that night was somehow comforting.

"Can you stay until I fall back asleep?"

I had expected him to say no and sling a smartass comment my way, but he surprised me that night. Sketchpad and pencil in one hand, he crawled into my bed without saying a word. *Oh my God...what about your points!* Stupid traitorous thoughts. Laces didn't lay down beside me; instead he chose to lean his back against the cool wall so he could draw with his sketchpad propped up in his lap.

What kind of punishment would we get for this anyway? I briefly wondered that as I took a calming breath and closed my eyes. The warmth that radiated from his skin underneath the covers was unbelievable. Our bodies were an inch apart, but I could still feel the heat from his leg as if it was tangled in mine.

I was halfway asleep when I heard his voice whisper soft ask, "What kind of books do you read?"

"What makes you think I read?"

I could hear his pencil stop. "Your wrists."

I yawned. "What about them?"

There was a long pause. "Scars like that make you want to escape the world."

Too tired to air any dirty laundry, I cuddled up to my pillow and sighed. "I love Wordsworth, Shakespeare, Emily

Bronte, Jane Austen…all of the oldies." I smiled into my pillow. "You're a fan of Emily Bronte."

I could hear him grinning as his pencil moved across the paper in smooth strokes. "Am I?"

"Mmm. You've mentioned Heathcliff before."

He barely tapped me with his foot. "Go to sleep."

"Nuh-uh. Not until you admit it." I teased. "I want to hear Hawthorne's bad boy admit that he is a Bronte fan."

Too set in his bad boy image, he refused, of course—and like the fainting spell he held over my head, I made a silent vow to hold Emily Bronte over his for the rest of eternity.

TWELVE

Gambrielle

"So...I gave Reyes a blowjob last night." Varla confessed the next morning in front of the bathroom mirror. "Don't look at me like that. It was an even exchange. Both parties left satisfied."

I spit my toothpaste into the sink. "I thought you said Thorne was the only guy worthy around here."

Varla proceeded to apply some mascara to her lashes. "Worthy, yes. Blowjob, no." She shrugged and did her left side. "My options were limited. I had to take what I could get."

I rinsed my toothbrush and stuck it back in the travel bag the ward provided for my hygiene products. "I wouldn't know anything about *that*." I admitted, flushing. "I've never been on an actual date or you know..." *Had sex...*

Varla capped her mascara and studied me via her reflection. Her blue hair was in high pigtails and when she chuckled they lightly bounced. "I'd like to say that I'm surprised by your confession, but I'm not. Strict parents?"

I nodded. "I don't think I actually spoke to a boy until my 5th grade project."

Varla laughed. "Were they afraid he would impregnate you with his crayons?" She shook her head and grabbed her travel bag. "Don't worry. You're not missing out on anything. Most men our age don't know how to use their equipment, and the ones that do can't find the right hole if they had Google Maps giving them directions ."

Something I'd learned in the short time I'd known her was she could always be counted on to liven up the conversation, and that included making me feel better about my sexual inexperience.

On the way to morning meds I thought about the previous night, about waking up to an empty bed that Laces had occupied with me; his warm legs sometimes touching my own as he shifted to get comfortable. I didn't want to like it—the friction I felt every time his body collided with mine—but it was hard to ignore. I'd never felt that sensation with anyone else. It was like my body was on fire, with nothing in sight to help extinguish the flames.

Did he tell anyone?

Was there really anything to tell? I found it odd that one of my greatest fears at Hawthorne had become my source of comfort.

Okay, don't look at him. Pay attention to the board, I thought to myself as Miss Maroon began her daily speech about the importance of goals. *I'll bet he plays footsie with Nurse Kline every night after they have—*

"Pssst."

What's this? I pried my eyes away from the goal list I started for the day—which included a few possible places my sister, Elizabeth, would hide her diary—and looked at Varla. Her hand was going strong on her notebook, a hint of pride crossing through her eyes as she scribbled what I could only imagine was a play-by-play of her and Reyes getting down to business in the janitor's closet....

There was a kick on the leg of my desk. *Ah, so he's the culprit*...propping my hand on my cheek, I turned to look at Laces—who was slumped down in his desk, biting the cap of his pen.

"What?" I whispered.

His lips spread into the biggest grin. "You hogged the bed."

My heart stopped with a loud thump and all of the color drained from my face. *Mayday! Mayday!* Could anyone hear this?

"I don't mind, but I figured you should know in case you ever decided to buy a bed." The cap of the pen tapped against his pearly whites almost rhythmically as his blue eyes dropped to my lips. *No!* Not here. A line needed to be drawn!

Blinking once, twice—I tore my eyes away from his bedroom eyes and attacked my journal with my pencil.

Another kick at the leg of my desk. I didn't look up this time, but I could feel his body moving closer. "If we're going to make this a regular thing, you're going to have to shave those legs." His smooth and seductive voice hung in the air as I flipped the page in my journal and started to write preparations for my funeral. *Gambrielle Evans was a brave soul...*

I felt like I was naked before a crowd of thousands of people.

What dignity I had was gone. Poof!

Another kick. *Oh God...*

"Please don't." I groaned. I was already embarrassed enough.

"Tonight's movie night. Rec room. 8 o'clock." There

was a hint of warning in his tone. "Don't forget to bring the *entertainment* with you."

Entertainment?

Luckily, I didn't have to wait long to figure out what he was referring to. A few minutes later, Varla tossed a note onto my desk, which explained everything for me.

ENTERTAINMENT=Your video monologue. A.K.A, clips from your trial. Nancy Grace interviews etc.

I quickly sent word back.

Why are we doing this? What's the point?

Varla rolled her eyes, scribbled something down, and passed the note back.

Trust me, it's fun! You'll die when you see Thorne's! He put Simpson's car chase to shame!

I turned to her and hissed. "I don't have a video, Varla." These weren't exactly memories I wanted to rehash.

"YouTube." Varla insisted.

I snorted. "I highly doubt anyone wants to watch the mascara running down my face."

"I do." Laces said from behind my shoulder, and I squeezed my eyes shut. *He would...*

"Think of it as initiation, okay?" Varla said in a chirpy voice. She closed her notebook and rose to her feet. "Everyone in the group has to go through this."

I gawked up at her. "Why?"

Were they sadists? I was beginning to wonder...

"Because...our group is family. And we protect our family." Varla said, offering a kind smile. "But we can't protect them from what we don't know, Gam."

Huh.

Well alright then...

My eyes fell. I didn't want them to see me crying and

begging for a judge to give me justice on Elizabeth's behalf. Laces already thought I was weak and video evidence would only confirm what he'd told me when we were alone in my room: that I was a people pleaser and weak for letting Joe walk all over me.

What would Varla think? Reyes? Thorne? I didn't know Reyes or Thorne very well, but something in my mind kept taunting me, insisting that this was the type of thing that would ruin any friendship I could've had with them.

I SKIPPED lunch in favor of going to the library to work on my video monologue. In order for me to get out of Hawthorne I needed to *survive* Hawthorne, and that started with formulating friendships.

They wanted to know my life, why I was there in the first place.

Okay...

But what if my tale of woe didn't meet their standards? Was there some type of list they checked off when deciding if you made the cut? Would I be too crazy, *or not crazy enough?*

Both Varla and Laces had been very vague when talking about the night's festivities. Pizza, soda, and candy were a given, as was public humiliation and shame apparently. I didn't know if there would be music, tissues— perhaps a therapist to help ease me into the situation?

Despite it being in a psych ward, the library smelled heavenly. New and old books filled the air, promising adventure, love, and betrayal. I desperately wanted to check out a few books on poetry—and maybe some of Shakespeare's greatest sonnets—but I wasn't there for that.

There were six laptops in the far corner. All empty. I took the one closest to the wall and quickly ventured down the rabbit hole known as YouTube. It occurred to me while hunting that if there were any videos of my darkest moment, then there were probably a few comments too. That alone sent a wave of panic crashing through me.

In the end Varla was right. *Typical.* Several videos were uploaded—including an interview I had given to a New York reporter on the third day of the trial. *Breathe. Breathe… you have to do this.*

I swallowed hard as the thumbnails of my face laughed back at me. This was the one and only time I wished I had taken my morning meds. Heart pounding, legs shaking, I put on the available headphones and click the mouse.

"Miss Evans, you say that you were abused by District Attorney Evans for the last ten years but that you didn't speak-up for fear of retaliation. What gave you the courage to finally take that extra step and report your stepfather?"

Dressed in a cream skirt and lavender top I walked past the glass windows of the courthouse with my attorney, Malcolm, ushering me through the crowd. The New York reporter followed behind like a lost puppy.

"Miss Evans?" The reporter pressed on.

I looked straight at the camera as we entered the parking lot. "My sister. She deserves justice and I intend to make sure that she gets it."

"Mr. Evans testified today that you have a history of self-harm—"

"—I have never cut myself!" I was past the point of irate and pushing people to get out of my way.

Oh God…

My finger pointed at every reporter in sight, "If you believe him you're nothing more an accessory to his ongoing torture and abuse! I did the right thing! I told you the truth! Why won't you help me?"

Tears pooled into my eyes as I stared at the eleven inch screen. Closing the laptop, I buried my face in my hands and took a deep breath. I was supposed to be getting justice for her, not playing house with a bunch of misfits. The image of Joe jerking down her panties blurred my vision. He was pissed, his menacing eyes glared at her bed as he grabbed a fistful of her blonde hair and jerked her head back.

I wasn't there in the library.

No.

I was back in the closet watching helplessly as he ripped off her shirt. I wanted to scream for him to stop, to grab the bat underneath the bed and finish what Elizabeth had once promised to do—but I couldn't move. At the sight of him thrusting inside of her my body went numb.

Breathe…

Squeezing my eyes shut I grabbed my chest and slowly rocked back and forth, begging for the air to come back to my lungs, all the while whispering the same phrase over and over: *You're mommy's little bumblebee. You're a bumblebee, yes you are. You're a bumblebee to the stars. You're a bumblebee, yes you are. You're mommy's little bumblebee.*

"Hey."

A soft shake came to my shoulder.

You should've helped her.

"Stray! Hey!"

My body shook involuntarily.

"Open your eyes!" The voice commanded. There was too much going on and I couldn't process who it was speaking to me.

"Go away." I stammered, hugging myself. *Go away Joe.* With tears coursing down my cheeks, I continued to rock.

And then a pair of strong hands cupped my cheeks. "Deep breath, come on. Pull yourself out of it!"

My teeth chattered. "He's coming after me."

"No!" The hands gave my head a rough shake in an attempt to stop the madness. "Let's talk about the bumblebee, alright? You're a bumblebee, yeah?"

"Bumblebee."I sobbed. The pain in my chest seemed to intensify with each passing second—and then as quickly as it came it vanished when a warm finger caressed the side of my cheek, sending an electric spark flowing through my body like quicksilver. I cracked my eyes open.

Laces was knelt down in front of me, his unruly black hair hanging in his eyes as he shook me again. There was worry roaming around his gorgeous blue gaze; a worry I'd never seen from any man before today.

"He's coming after me!" I wailed, throwing my arms around his back. His muscular arms wrapped around me so tight, I thought my lungs would burst… "He did it, Lincoln. He killed her!"

Resting his chin on my shoulder, Laces stroked the back of my head as though I were a child. "It's okay." he soothed.

"I can't do this!" Everyone else had abandoned me to the ward. I had no one.

Laces placed a soft kiss on my forehead. "Shhh, bumblebee."

THIRTEEN

Laces

"I HEAR INITIATION IS TONIGHT." Nurse Kline tossed a chocolate peanut into her mouth and winked. We were in her personal office hidden away from prying eyes. Her sweet voice, which I had once thought would be my saving grace in this hellhole, didn't sound so sweet anymore; there was an unspoken threat behind her playful urgency, a tension that I couldn't place.

Giving a curt nod, I bit into my apple and slowly began to chew as she did a once over of me sprawled out on the suede sofa. The window was right beside me and the heat from the sun's midday rays felt good against my chilled skin. Of everything in the ward there was to bitch about— no cell phones and lack of privacy—my constant complaint was always the temperature. Because of germs the staff was required to keep the thermostat at fifty-five degrees at all times, which made for some chilly nights. Throwing my arm behind my head, I eyed Nurse Kline's expectant gaze. I sighed. "What?"

"I want to know what your plan is." Nurse Kline clasped her hands together and propped them under her chin, a vindictive smile spreading across her thin lips as she urged me on. "Thorne could keep guard at the doors and *you can do what you do*."

Do what you do…

I stopped chewing on my apple and narrowed my gaze. What she was speaking of—the dark path that had at one point consumed my every waking thought and most of my unconscious ones too—those of which had been buried for so long. "You can't be serious." I murmured dryly.

"Oh, come on, Laces. Don't you miss seeing the fear in someone's eyes? The rush?" Her voice dropped to barely a whisper as she teased, "Being in full control? Having someone at your mercy?"

"No." I muttered. There was more force than I intended behind my words, but oh well. She was basically asking me to awaken a demon, a demon I wasn't sure I would be able to put back to bed once it came out to play, and I couldn't do that. Not to *her*. Seeing the disappointment welling into Nurse Kline's eyes, I tossed what remained of my apple into the trashcan beside her desk and decided now was as good a time as any to bail from this fucked-up charade that I'd been a part of for, oh, the last four-eight hours. Coming up behind her desk, I held onto her desk for support and seductively leaned forward until we were an inch apart. "You don't want to share me with anyone else, do you baby? Let's cut the shit and go back to the way things were." Yes, more fuckin', less plotting. Her pussy and my dick would be sated, and at night she would go home and fake an orgasm for Kenny. From where I was looking it was a win-win for both of us. *Yes, I like this plan very much*…it didn't have Gambrielle anywhere in the equation, which was an added bonus. The thought of the poor girl enduring any misfortunes at my expense put an awful taste in my mouth.

Before I had the opportunity to delve into the big details and really sell the idea, Nurse Kline decided she wanted to be boss—she reached forward and grabbed my throat. She was about to give it a hard squeeze, but I was too quick. Mimicking her gesture, I jerked forward and wrapped my hand around her neck too. I squeezed hard, my fingers turning white around her sun-kissed flesh. Lifting her up by the neck, I pressed my lips against her ear as she furtively gasped for air. "You forget who's running this circus!" I hissed into her ear.

She cried out—her bloodshot eyes pleading with me. She knew better; and if she didn't she would after today. Keeping a firm hold on her neck, I shuffled through her desk searching for my weapon of choice. They didn't keep knives at Hawthorne—which was a pity, because I was an inpatient man and it was a lot easier to get my point across with a sharp, shiny blade. "Pencils, pens, post-its, paper-clips…" My narrow eyes flickered back to my prey, "We can do better than that, can't we?"

What air she had left she used to get out a strangled "Please…"

Pathetic.

"Shhh, baby. It'll be over soon." I chuckled. Spotting a nail-file, my eyes lit up at all of the possibilities. "It's no machete, but it'll do in a pinch." Pressing the sharp tip against her smooth neck, I watched in awe as she flinched. She was shaking, her lips turning blue, but that was the least of my worries. With my lips back at her ear, I whispered "I thought we had an understanding, hmm?"

We do. We do. We do. She mouthed over and over as tears welled into her eyes. *I'm sorry.*

"I'm not one of your orderlies that you can order and command like a mindless Gollum." I seethed. As Nurse Kline's eyes began to roll back an epiphany overwhelmed me, knocking the wind right out of my lungs: I needed survival, but at the moment my survival was dependent on a southern belle whose issues seemed more dire than my own. Call it sympathy, a case of feelings, or whatever the hell you like. All I knew was I could not subject a poor, defensive, naïve girl to anymore torture than she was already living. Her stepfather had taken the title for Top Bastard, and all I could hope for was a chance at being her Top Friend and I was riding a thin line at that.

So…

I loosened my grip on her neck and pushed the nail-file further into her skin, until a steady stream of blood trickled down her chest. My nostrils flared and my cock hardened at the beautiful sight. I was confused—part of my brain was telling me I had already made my bed, that I needed to accept that this was my life. The other part, A.K.A, the angel tapping my right shoulder with its halo, saw a chance for a do-over, a future, an opportunity to start a fresh life away from Hawthorne's iron gates.

"Lin-coln." Nurse Kline stammered. "Please!"

Why do you care so much for the stray?

Was what I was doing, caring? Uncertain, I shook my head and licked my dry lips. A year ago I wouldn't have been caught dead doing this to Nurse Kline; we didn't have a future, both of us knew that, and yet I still yearned for her, for the comfort of someone who knew me front to back and could accept my faults without judgement.

Stray doesn't accept you.

But could she?

That was the question of the hour.

I looked back at Nurse Kline, at the terror swirling around in her drab brown eyes as she continued to whisper soothing pleas of apologies. Her tears, as beautiful as they were falling from her cheeks, didn't have the same effect on me as Gambrielle's. *Not even close...* and that was the real epiphany for my black soul.

"Leave her alone." I ordered, still holding the nail-file to her neck. I didn't need to tell her who to leave alone, she was a smart girl and put two-and-two together real quick. "Do your damn job and fix her or I swear to God..." She had seen bits and pieces of the damage I left in my wake, but she didn't know the true destruction I was capable of. I jerked away and shoved the contraband nail-file in my scrub pocket, carefully watching a terrified Nurse Kline as I made my way to the door.

Calm down.

It's over.

You did her a justice.

I didn't think Nurse Kline had it in her to give a snarly retort, but boy was I wrong. "She's never going to love you, not like I do. I know you, I know how you think. She doesn't." She paused, "what do you think she'll say when she finds out about Lexi?"

What would she say? Would she understand?

Probably not.

Which was why she was never going to find out about her; I'd see to that right now.

Smirking, I put my hand up to my ear, "What's that, officer? Nurse Kline slept with underage boys, what?" I taunted. The same fear from before returned to her eyes, and I couldn't help the sense of pride that filled my chest. If she didn't know who she was dealing with before, she did now. Holding my arms out, I bowed, then kissed two fingers and blew a smartass kiss to seal her fate.

"Laces!" It was a desperate plea.

There was no room for mercy. "It started when I was sixteen." A demented chuckle slipped through my lips as I stepped in the hallway and turned to close the door. "I told her no, but she had all of this power, officer." I winked as I opened the door and stepped out into the hallway. "Don't forget your place."

TELLING Thorne and Reyes that I had screwed up the sweet deal we had at Hawthorne was ten times worse than anything Nurse Kline had thrown at me. For two, almost three years, we had lived like kings amongst the patients here, and now we were about to lose all of our special privileges—weekend alcohol parties in Thorne's room, cigarettes, a pussy to fuck whenever we needed a release; it all came with the package deal of being Nurse Kline's favorite.

She would most likely keep Thorne because, *he was Thorne*...She admired his strange fuckery and what it encompassed: whips, chains, do-it-yourself-pornos.

But Reyes?

Reyes didn't stand a chance in the world.

Thirty minutes before the entertainment was set to start in the rec room, I finally worked up the nerve to inform them of the impending change that was likely to happen in the coming weeks. Knowing that they wouldn't accept a simple "I was bored of her", I created a storyline to help feed their egos, but also to get them to side with me.

"She wants a foursome? Why?" Reyes shouted, arranging the USB drives on the flat screen shelf.

"There goes my alcohol." Thorne quipped, circling a word in his crossword puzzle. He didn't look up from where he sat in front of the TV.

"Let's not panic." I said, peeking out the door. Varla and Gambrielle were nowhere in sight.

"This is because of Evans, isn't it?" Reyes asked. He was too smart for his own good. When I didn't answer he shook his head in dismay, "I knew it. I knew she would screw-up everything we've worked for." He'd been against her from the beginning.

Thinking the truth might win me a little favor, I explained what Nurse Kline had wanted me to do so she could secure a fourth floor. It worked on Thorne—he muttered a few curses and slammed his crossword puzzle book shut. Reyes, however, was torn.

Varla and Gambrielle showed up right at eight o'clock. Both handed Reyes their USB drives and his somber eyes stayed locked on Gambrielle for far longer than was appropriate. He didn't know what to make of her or the situation she'd brought.

Thorne's exposé was always the most entertaining, so Varla felt he needed to go first.

Okay.

As long as Gambrielle wasn't falling apart I had no qualms. As Thorne plugged his USB into the right port, Reyes cocked his head toward me and whispered, hissing "Does she even like you??!!!"

"Not for now." I muttered through the corner of my lips.

"What if she bats for the other team, hmm? Have you thought about that?" He eagerly tapped my shoulder in a desperate attempt to get my attention. "You might be putting us through all of this hell for nothing!"

I shot him a deadly gaze. "Not. Now."

"I'm just sayin…"

"Say less."

Before Thorne began his entertainment, he turned to face his audience and pushed his long, blonde hair away from his face. With his attention solely on Gambrielle, he flashed one of his charming, boyish smiles, and said, "Hey Gambrielle, my name is Thorne Walsh, and I'm from Venice, California."

Reyes' voice was back at my ear, "Why does he sound like a contestant on The Bachelorette?"

He made a valid point.

"I like surfing, and I hate shirts." Thorne chuckled. Varla whistled for him to show his *washboard abs* but he ignored her, keeping his full attention on the newbie in the room.

Now it was my turn to cock my head in Reyes' direction. "I'm going to need a cigarette for this." He slapped a lighter and cigarette in my hand and I wasted no time lighting up. Taking a long draw of the sweet nicotine, I snapped my fingers and gestured for Thorne to wrap-up his speech. I was ready to show Gambrielle what the boys of Hawthorne were made of.

FOURTEEN

Gambrielle

"BREAKING NEWS OF THE HOUR: the boyfriend of murder victim, Stacey Hurd, has been arrested and charged with suspicion of murder. This comes four days after Hurd's body was found abandoned in a Los Angeles warehouse. Reporter Tamara Poe has more. Tamara?"

A woman appeared on the flat screen, her perfectly manicured pointer finger directing attention to the brick warehouse behind her. "That's right, Dan. I'm here at what used to be the most popular floral shop in town, Floral Bay Creations. It's hard to believe but two years ago this building was the go-to leader for wedding bouquets; women across the world traveled to this location to see the hundreds of arrangements created weekly by Jan Bay."

Murder at an floral shop?

Dear Lord...cold chills went down my spine.

"Stacey Hurd, an aspiring ballerina from San Francisco, was found hanging from a closet on the second floor. There was no suicide note, and her family says there was no indication of any mental illness. They say she was a quiet soul who spent most of her free time in a dance studio."

An older woman, who I assumed was Stacey's mother, appeared on screen. "She had everything to live for—which was why we found it so odd that she had taken her own life. I just couldn't wrap my mind around what happened. Even after the detective told me his findings, I shook my head and said *no, not my Stacey*."

I took a generous sip of my soda and forced a smile at Thorne, who was reciting each word from memory. *Omg…* my soda caught in my throat and I coughed—which earned me a soft pat on the back from Laces.

This was a bad idea.

Really bad.

I looked back at the screen. A photo of a ballerina with long, black hair, and a trim waist faded in and out. "Everything was going fine until she met *him*." Her mother said.

"By him, Stacey's mother was referring to model, Thorne Walsh. The two had met in early 2016 and became inseparable, with Stacey often telling her mother that Walsh was *the one*."

"He had the looks, money—um, a nice condo in the city." Stacey's mother said, wiping away a tear. "Anything she wanted, he gave her."

"That included a full ride to California University, a flashy Mercedes, and her own credit cards to spend to her heart's desire." Reporter Tamara Poe said. Images of shiny cars, stock footage of a university campus and candid shots of Stacey toasting at an elaborate birthday party entered the screen. "So what went wrong?"

I waited with baited breath for Tamara to explain, hoping and praying that maybe there was some kind of misunderstanding. Maybe they were doing this to me as a joke? But then the clip cut to Thorne sitting in a well-lit room with a reporter named Carlos. "Did you kill Stacey Hurd?" he asked.

Thorne rubbed his chin thoughtfully, as though he hadn't a care in the world. "Define kill."

My breath caught.

"Did you put a noose around Stacey's neck and push her off of a chair?"

"No." Thorne's voice was very even as he spoke. "Did I say things to her to promote the suicide—Yes." He didn't bat a lash. "I'm not going to be polite and mince words when someone I love says, *Thorne, I'm pregnant with your best friend's child, we're going to get married...*"

The reporter held up his finger. "So she cheated, but did she deserve to die for it?"

Thorne shrugged. "Did I deserve to be cheated on?"

"It's not the same." The reporter argued.

"I beg to differ. She put me through hell, and now she's in hell." Thorne crossed one leg negligently over the other and smiled back at the reporter. "The only reason I am being thrown shade is because I'm being honest. Honesty scares people."

The reporter quickly clapped back, "or maybe you're crazy?"

Thorne didn't miss a beat. Flashing a brilliant smile he nodded, "Maybe, I guess that's for the court of popular opinion to decide."

With each passing minute I became morally torn about Thorne's past. Stacey—God rest her soul—had been living the high life from model, Thorne Walsh. She had everything, except what she really wanted, his best friend. And now she was six feet under because of her stupid decision. Wait, that's awful to say, isn't it? My features screwed up as I looked at Varla, who was throwing back chips like they were going out of style.

"Pssst."

She leaned toward me.

"I don't know how I feel about this. I want to feel pity for the poor girl but…" I trailed off and looked back at the screen, which now had a photograph from Stacey's funeral being shoved in Thorne's face by the reporter. Thorne waved him off like an insect and the entire room broke out in laughter.

"That is the best part." Reyes caroused as he clapped his hands. "He's going to suffocate you with the funeral YOU PAID FOR Thorne!"

Hmmm… I chewed on my lower lip. "What am I supposed to be feeling right now?" I blurted out. Thorne paused the clip. "I guess what I want—no, need to know—is do you feel um, the slightest bit bad for pushing her over the edge?" *Yes, that's a good way to put it*. He had driven poor Stacey to madness until she couldn't take it anymore.

Thorne and Laces exchanged glances, and then Laces gave him permission to explain—which I found out technically wasn't allowed, but they were making an exception tonight.

Propping his elbows on his knees Thorne shrugged, "She didn't need anyone else. She had me."

My heart picked up some speed. "Ohhh-kay, but…"

"She could've been honest and told me the truth, she didn't, and she paid with her life for it."

"Thorne hates liars." Varla said.

"Yeah but…you didn't just aid in her suicide, you aided in the death of a baby." I said, stunned. I couldn't believe the words falling out of my lips; the fact that I was having this conversation, period, seemed surreal.

"She should've thought about that before she fucked him in my bed." Thorne muttered. There was no getting through to him, I knew. No matter how horrible, he was set in his ways and reasons. And as bad as I hated to admit it, I pitied him—like truly pitied him.

"I'm sorry." I finally whispered, glancing down at my lap. My knotted up hands were as white as snow. I was anxious, on edge, and feeling somewhat sick about everything.

I got up from my seat.

"I don't want to see anymore videos. All it does is paint you in a bad light." I shook my head. "If you want me to know what you did then just say it—don't be afraid to be honest."

Reyes held up his finger. "The clips refer to us as sexy and mysterious."

Laces nodded, clearly agreeing with his friend. "It evens out all of the bad shit we did."

"Absolutely." There was a fierceness to Reyes' tone, like he was willing to fight to the death to keep entertainment night alive. "In here we're nobodies." He pointed at the window hidden behind a bookshelf in the corner. "Out there, they respect us. They know better to mess with us."

Thorne nodded hard. This was something everyone, even Varla, agreed on. They didn't care if people thought they were crazy for what they did—all they cared about was the recognition and respect that followed.

"My video isn't going to be as elaborate as any of yours." I said, folding my arms. "And I don't care how pissed off any of you get for this but—the only reason I'm in here is because I told the truth." No one spoke. I explained what had happened—the abuse I had endured, my sister's rape, and my gathering the courage to speak to someone. "I did the right thing and I still ended up here. Where's the justice in that, Thorne? Laces? Reyes? Varla? Do you think it's fair that a rapist sleeps comfortably every night, while I'm bound by the state of North Carolina to be here?"

When no one spoke, I scoffed and stormed out, cursing every name in the book as I stomped down the hallway. In an attempt to feel better I made a pit stop at the library and snatched a hard copy of Wuthering Heights off the shelf before going to my room. Breathing heavy, I crawled into my bed and opened the book, ready to escape to a kinder world—well, kinder to me; one that made sense in all-of-this ruckus.

A pair of knuckles knocked against my door a few minutes later. I knew who it was, but chose not to acknowledge his presence. I don't know why, but I had expected more from him—not an angel by any means, but a friend.

"I fucked up." he said right as I was turning the page. "I shouldn't have forced you to watch any of it."

Be strong. I took a deep breath. He needed to atone for his sins, and me smiling while he made a big elaborate—and possibly heartfelt speech—would only deter the progress he had made. "I'm listening." I mumbled.

He moved closer. "You were right: I am a fan of Emily Bronte. She was my mother's favorite writer."

Oh? At that I couldn't help but glance up from my book. He had never spoken a word about his mom, so this was a pretty big step. "Was she an artist?"

Sitting down at the edge of my bed, he shook his head. "No, she was a nurse. My father was the artist." Putting my book aside, I crawled to where he was and for a while there was nothing but the strident sound of our breaths to keep us company. He interlaced his hand with mine and gave a soft squeeze; I felt the same as before, like an electric current was coursing through my body, lighting every nerve ending on fire. The ache formed low in my belly and moved down my thighs, causing me to cross my legs to ease the sensation.

I knew I was turned on.

I'd been sheltered from most things in life, but *not this*. My P.E. instructor had given us *the talk* the first week of freshman year, and my mother, not wanting to have any grandchildren just yet, had followed suit and voiced what she knew in the weeks that followed.

My breasts felt heavy, my panties were wet…

He needs to leave.

But he wasn't.

So in order to avoid looking like a bigger fool I took the road far less traveled by girls like me.

"If I tell you something will you promise not to hold it against me?" I asked, clenching my thighs together.

With our hands still laced together, he turned to face me and my breathing grew heavy as the grin I'd come to know so well spread across his lips. "I won't hold it against you—but I can't promise not to laugh." He warned.

"I'll take what I can get." My eyes fell to my feet. I took a deep breath to calm my nerves. "I don't know how to explain it without feeling stupid. Ugh."

"Do you want to write it down and give it to me?"

I frowned. "I wouldn't know how to phrase it, exactly."

He blinked.

"Please just," I paused, "don't make fun of me for it, okay? I've never talked about this before so I don't know the protocol for this type of thing."

"Alright, I promise I won't make fun of you." I'd piqued his interest.

"Okay." I squeezed my eyes shut. He was still holding my hand, which was a good thing, right? *Absolutely.* He hadn't bailed on me for anything else, so surely he would understand this. I squeezed his hand, hard. "I have this ache in my um…"

Damn. I rarely ever cursed but this situation demanded it. *Damn.*

"In your…"

I cracked my eyes to see Laces zoned out staring at my lap.

"Do I have to spell it out?" I whispered.

His hungry eyes flashed to me. "Yes." He rasped.

Glancing away, I swallowed the dryness in my throat. "My um—*AREA*—is in a bit of discomfort." I said carefully. "And I'm not going to look at you right now because it'll only make it worse. Can you leave, please? I'm not mad, I'm just agitated."

I expected to hear his footsteps making tracks for the door at any second, but karma didn't give me that reprieve.

"Look at me." Laces said quietly, giving my hand a light squeeze.

I couldn't.

Something was wrong with me. It had to be. Physically, Laces was the ideal male specimen; he was tall and lean, with gorgeous blue eyes and stunningly high cheekbones that rivaled most models. Only a fool would've turned him down.

I guess I was that fool.

"Please don't do this to me. Can't you seem I am embarrassed beyond belief?" I said. I released his hand and jumped to my feet, pacing back and forth like a manic as he lay back in my bed and threw his sculpted arms behind his head, watching my every move. I pressed the palm of my hand into my upper thigh, "God, when does it stop?!"

"I can fix it for you."

What?!!?? "No, no thank you."

"I'll be quick." His voice—God—the way the words fell so seductively off his sinful lips.

Stopping at the foot of my bed, I finally took a moment to really look at him. He was comfortable?—and not at all affected by my confession. His blue eyes were hazy and full of want; add in the way he was sprawled out, legs a foot apart, and his hoodie barely covering the V-crease of his hip and you had the perfect combination for swoon worthy eye candy.

I pointed at his eyes. "Stop looking at me."

"Come on, baby. Don't be like that."

"Baby? Don't—what?" I fisted my hands through my hair. "What is going on right now—are you trying to seduce me?"

He cracked a smile. "That depends: do you want to be seduced?"

Do you? Did I?

"You're not attracted to me though. Remember?" I was frantic.

His eyes drifted shut and I can't explain it, the sense of overwhelming dread that entered my soul when he finally opened his eyes again and looked at me. "I lied."

My lips parted. This was a first. "You're attracted to me?"

"Mmmm."

I blurted out the first thing that came to mind: "So, what?—you're imagining my face while getting off to Nurse Kline?" Whatever comfort he had felt evaporated instantly. The bed, which he'd gotten cozy on, suddenly became a pit of lava and he jumped up so fast. "Yeah, did you honestly think I would forget about her? That I would just spread my legs for you?"

I could see the war raging in his eyes as he grabbed my chin and forced me to look at him. "That's over."

I scoffed.

"It is!" He growled.

I smacked his hand away, "Don't you shout at me!"

He fisted his hands through his hair, gripping the black ends so tightly. "We can discuss this later—right now I want to give you an orgasm."

"Ah!"

He truly was shameless.

"There's a janitor's closet down the hallway, right across from the men's room." Laces said. "Meet me there in ten minutes and I'll rectify your *situation*."

"No."

Laces' jaw clenched. "I wasn't asking for your permission."

"Good, because you're not going to get it!" I snapped. Spinning on one heel, I marched to my bed and crawled under the sheets. This night needed to end, quickly, before I died from humiliation. "Please just go!"

Yeah, and take that sexy milk-can-do-a- body-good torso with you!

The pain, though constantly uncomfortable in his presence, was bearable. I wasn't desperate enough to shack up in the dirty old janitor's room. *Not yet.* Hearing his footsteps retreating to the hallway, I breathed out a sigh of relief and squeezed my eyes shut, willing sleep to take over.

FIFTEEN

Laces
───────────

Denied?

My poor cock. He didn't ask for much: a clean pair of drawers, a shower, a hand to keep him warm—and to be fed. Basic needs, people. And now, Gambrielle Evans had taken away one of the essentials for survival, dinner.

Out of respect for my cock—as well as my own sanity—I ignored Gambrielle in the days that followed. I needed time to strategize and regroup, and also to mourn the orgasm that never was. Men outside of Hawthorne would've thrown back a few shots, screwed a slut or two in a bar, and maybe took a picture of their erect cock and sent it to the enemy to give them a taste of what they were missing.

But not here.

In a psych ward the game was more complex. All attacks had to be covert and carefully executed for maximum damage.

"I could've gotten myself off, but what's the fun in that?" I blasted days later in one-on-one therapy. "She knew what she was doing, leading my cock into the black abyss!" I slammed my fist on his desk, shaking his cup of pens and paper clips. "How is he supposed to ever trust her again?"

"You mean *you*." Dr. Young corrected.

I grabbed a handful of my cock and gave it a healthy shake, "No, him! He is his own entity! I bring my hair gel and condoms—and that's it! He's the one making serious plays!" Couldn't he see the position I was now in? The turmoil my body was facing at the hands of the simpering southern belle, *fuck*, it would take months, if not years, to recoup the dignity my cock had lost! Pushing my hair away from my face, I glared at Dr. Young as he tried to make sense of it all. "And do you know what else pisses me off, Doc?"

Dr. Young peeked up from his jotting notes down on his ever present legal pad. "You didn't get a blowjob?"

I threw my head back and laughed, the inky strands of my hair falling into my eyes as I pointed at him. "That's a good one, but no." I straightened and slowly leaned forward, meeting Dr. Young at the center of his desk. "I would've eaten that pussy all night long, no questions asked."

"I don't follow. Most men enjoy—"

"—I don't eat pussy!!!!" I shouted.

Silence filled the small confinements of his room.

Pussy was like food, and I was a *picky eater*.

Always had been.

But with Gambrielle I didn't have to mull over the menu and check the ingredients to decide if she was worth my time. *No*. I already knew she would be. She had an aroma about her, a sweet scent that obstructed everything in its path long after she had gone, making it impossible to select anything else.

Dr. Young rocked back and forth in his seat. I could see

it in his eyes, his mind reeling from my confession as he tried to decide whether or not to up my medication, or blame it on a hormonal imbalance. "Would you hurt this girl to get her—FRUIT?"

"Maybe." Hey, at least I was honest!

More silence, then a "What does that mean?!!!"erupted from the good doctor.

"It means I need that pussy, dumbass!"

Dr. Young squeezed his eyes shut and took a deep breath before whispering, "Please promise me you will behave appropriately on this week's outing to Baylor."

Every two weeks the ward allowed us to go shopping in one of the neighboring counties. This week the mall in Baylor had offered to host us for four hours. It was supposed to be a constructive exercise, one to help ease us back into polite society. But truth be told there were more tears than dollars actually spent.

"I can only speak for myself—not my cock." I snickered. "He's cooking up some big plans down there."

Dr. Young shook his head. "Then maybe you should sit this one out." He tried to be nice about it, patting my hand and all that bullshit.

"I can't do that."

Dr. Young ran his hands down his face, clawing at his pores, and groaned. "Oh why not?!" He demanded.

"Because this is the first time in a year that I've been eligible for a weekend pass and I'd… like to get out for a while." I kept my voice even as his eyes widened to the size of lemons. He didn't know what to think about this, or the pussy drought—hell, any of it, really. I'd thrown so much at him in the last hour that I was surprised he didn't pull his wig off.

"You're joking with me, right?" Dr. Young chuckled after a minute of uninterrupted silence. "No one in their right mind would give you a free pass home. You're a FLIGHT RISK."

I cracked a smile and proudly stated, "I've behaved."

He snorted. "No, you haven't been caught. Keyword: caught." Frustrated, he shuffled through the papers on his desk until he found a bright pink one. He handed it to me. "Since you were admitted by the state of North Carolina there is a specific protocol we have to follow to maintain government funding at this facility. This will need to be filled out by your acting power of attorney."

Shit…

"My brother?"

"He is the power of attorney on your file. If Nurse Kline gives you the weekend pass I'll expect a detailed report from him next Monday."

I had planned on staying at my condo downtown, but Dr. Young blew that idea out of the water when I asked about it. "You are mentally unstable and therefore mentally unfit to be home alone." he said, checking something off. "You also have a lot of money, Laces. The last thing I need is a phone call from your father informing me that you blew your inheritance on strippers." When I didn't say anything his voice grew serious. "You're very blessed creatively and financially. In ten years I want to see your work in a museum, not in a psych ward."

THE RADIO SILENCE between Gambrielle and I lasted for four days. I could've held off for five or six, but my cock wasn't having it. Her pussy called to him like a siren's song, and he was more than willing to walk into the depths of her sea, even if it meant his death.

I'd planned on sitting with Cynthia Miles during the

trip to Baylor; she had promised me a blowjob in Bed, Bath, and Beyond, and I'd promised to hold her hand at the mall to seal the deal.

Cynthia would get her moment to shine, and my cock would empty out the load that was meant for Gambrielle. It seemed like a happy ending for everyone involved.

"You are not getting on this bus without a buddy!" The day orderly shouted as he escorted us past the nurse's station and through the main exit. "You will be responsible for your buddy and vice versa! You ain't gotta hold hands, but you will look out for one another!"

Where was Cynthia? Everyone was dressed in regular garb so it should've made the process of elimination easier. It didn't. I squeezed through the crowd, searching for a platinum blonde head with big lips and a killer ass.

"Hey."

It was her. Gambrielle.

Fuck.

I cracked a smile, but didn't look in her direction. She could drool over me all she wanted—but after two hand jobs and a raging blister, I'd learned my lesson. "Not now, stray. I'm busy."

"Are you really going to continue ignoring me?" Gambrielle asked in that angelic, innocent voice I adored. She tugged at the black t-shirt I'd worn. "I thought we had an understanding."

"We did," I said, and then hummed under my breath, "*Cock-blocker.*" I continued to scan the sea of patients for my prey. Cynthia was at the front of the bus talking to a patient from Floor A.

"Please don't do this." Gambrielle said. She knew exactly what I was about to do. Coming up from behind, she shot me a pained look and swallowed hard, her brown eyes pleading for some type of reason. A stabbing sensation started in my chest and worked its way down to my abs, wreaking hell on my entire body. I hadn't anticipated this reaction, so I wasn't sure how to handle it. "Whatever this is between us, if you do *this*, there's no going back. It's unforgivable, Lincoln."

I shook my head. "This is who I am." I muttered.

"The guy that goes and sleeps with whoever he wants when he doesn't get his way?"

I cringed. The analogy seemed a lot worse coming from her lips than it had from Dr. Young's.

"All you're going to do is prove me right." Gambrielle stated.

My eyes drew into slits. "It's. My. Life."

"It is." she agreed.

"Let me live it."

She nodded, her eyes falling to the pink ballet flats covering her feet. "I'm going to. But I want to tell you something before you do whatever it is you're planning to do…"

I tilted my head back and groaned at the sky. "And what's that?"

"You're an idiot, Lincoln Caster." Her voice was soft, but firm. "You can't see the good even when it's staring you right in the face."

Okay, that little snide comment hurt, bad. Perhaps if it had come from someone else I wouldn't have taken it so personally. My eyes dropped to her face as my defenses rose. "Watch your mouth." I warned. "Favorite or not, you're still in my domain."

Damn straight.

"Favorite? So there's more than one?" The pain that shot through her eyes in that moment was something that would haunt me for the rest of my days. I wanted to reach out—to hold her, assure her that everything would work out as it was supposed to—but I couldn't. I didn't have those emotions in me, and if I did I'm not sure I would've known how to use them, anyway.

Her face had paled to that of a wrath; her eyes were as glossy as a reflection in the sea.

I'd gone too far and needed to reel myself back in before I caused irreparable damage. Reaching forward I roughly grabbed her chin and whispered, reassuringly "Hey, there is no one else."

The tears continued to swim around in her brown irises, desperately searching for a lifeboat, an oar, something to grab on to… "Please don't do this."

She was referring again to Cynthia, who was currently making her way through the crowd.

Fuck.

I released Gambrielle's face.

"I can't—" I started.

"Why?"

"—because I don't know if I'll be able to wait that long!" I all but shouted. "And what if I can't, hmm?" Confusion entered her eyes but I didn't stop there. I'd already made my grave, or so I thought, so it was best to dig a deeper hole and lay in it. Leaning forward, I whispered into her ear, "There will come a point when I'll get tired of waiting and I'll take it with or without your consent. Is that what you want?!?!"

Goodbye Gambrielle—

"From you? Maybe!" She harshly whispered into my ear.

And….what the fuck is happening right now?

"Don't tempt me." I warned, pulling back. The heat raging in my groin seemed to grow as she lifted a shoulder, taunting me. There was tension all around us, a hate and lust that had finally reached a fever pitch. Flashing a coy smile, she swirled her finger around a long brunette strand hanging over her shoulder.

"I'm used to being forced to do things." Her cheeks flushed crimson as the words slipped out of her mouth. My cock instantly responded, the fabric tightening to the point of pain as my cock tested the structural integrity of my pants.

And in the midst of our heated exchange, the unthinkable happened—Cynthia bounced up to me, her lips puckering like a blowfish; without a second thought I planted my palm on her face and pushed her way. "I'm not playing around, Stray." I said. Cynthia's hands were wildly attacking the air, desperately trying to slap the hell outta my face. *Ease-up bitch!*

Gambrielle's lips spread into an adorable smile as she threw her thumb over her shoulder, "We could be buddies if you want and sit together on the bus? Maybe discuss it in more detail over lunch?" she asked, as a hopeful gleam entered her eyes.

"Are you asking me out?" After everything I had just said? Now it was my turn to look like an idiot.

Her brown eyes slowly fell. There was a little hesitation when she spoke again. "Yes?"

SIXTEEN

Gambrielle

"I SHOULDN'T HAVE to say this, but after what happened at our last outing in Charlotte I feel it is my responsibility as your teacher and friend," Miss Maroon's cheeks heated up as she stumbled over her statement, "to um, to tell you that it is a health hazard and safety risk to have sex with another patient in a department store. I know some of you have urges an-and needs—but nothing good can come from a poor grandmother seeing your bare gluteus maximus plastered against the glass entry of a JCPenny's. Right Mr. Park?" Her eyes shot to Reyes, who was beaming with such pride. "Right, Mr. Park?"

The bus went over a speed bump, but that didn't stop Reyes Sun Park from rising to his feet and placing his hand on his heart. "Thank you, Miss Maroon for that fine commentary." He cooed. "I'd also like to thank my co-star, Varla English, for taking care of me during that dark time. The window was cold, but her pussy kept me warm!"

The entire bus broke out in applause.

Turning to my right, I opened my mouth to say something to Varla who was way ahead of me. "Back to December had just been released and I was emotional." She explained. *Oh Varla...Why?*

Mouth still wide open, I shook my head as she continued on, the elaborate tale turning stranger as the seconds passed. "We went to Chinese before and...you know the chopsticks they give you for your meal?"

I blinked, dumbfounded. *Chopsticks?*

"Well, he um," She bit her lip to suppress a giggle, "he wanted to do some kinky shit with them, and one thing led to another—and don't you dare judge me, Gambrielle Evans!" Her eyes flew over my shoulder, to the gorgeous man sketching behind me. "I haven't said a thing about your Laces infatuation."

Jesus...did he hear that?

I stole a quick glance over my shoulder as the bus merged onto the highway. Laces had his head propped against the window, immersed in the sketch he was drawing of a hand. He looked like a runway model— ripped jeans, white tee, red and black long sleeved flannel shirt tightly secured around his waist. Most men couldn't pull off the high-fashion grunge look, but he did it effort-lessly. *And the black hair, God...*I licked my dry lips and quickly turned back to Varla, who was now grinning like she knew a secret. Patting the seat beside her, she stated, "It's time for girl talk."

I flushed. "There is nothing to talk about."

"Oh, I can think of plenty." Varla chirped, pulling me into her seat. She wasted no time getting down to the nitty gritty. "Who made the first move?"

Hmm...

"Me?"

Varla's eyes popped out like a cartoon character. "No!"

She all but shouted, and then calmly added, "Don't give him that power so early in the game!"

"What power?"

"Exactly! He doesn't have any because he made the first move!" Varla said with a finality in her voice that made me shiver. She had worn a short fluffy skirt with ruffles and a loose black tank. I thought it did a great job of complimenting her bright blue pixie cut. She reached for my hand, "If he wants sex you make sure he goes down for dinner first. He needs to stir the pot before adding any more ingredients. Capeesh?"

I rubbed my temples. "Oh my God…"

"Don't oh my God me, I'm giving you a basic rundown of what you deserve." She held her head up high, the butterfly clips in her blue hair twinkling against the morning sun. It was only then that I realized how out of place I felt sitting next to her in my school-girl esque uniform. "They are men first and psych patient's second—remember that. It'll keep you from feeling bad when he starts begging."

And that was pretty much what the ride to Baylor consisted of: Sex Etiquette 101, taught by Hawthorne's very own Varla English. Ten minutes before we arrived at the mall, I slipped back beside Laces and flashed an awkward smile when he looked up at me with a daunting gaze. "Sorry, Varla wanted to chat. You know how she gets." I whispered.

His eyes—*dear Jesus*—they stripped my soul with one look. He tucked his pencil behind his ear and reached forward—caressing the side of my cheek as though I were the most fragile object in the world—and whispered "I don't beg Stray, *but you will*."

My breath hitched in my lungs.

His smooth finger slowly trailed over my lips, tracing

each groove and indention and committing it to memory. It was a strange feeling, the fleeting comfort of his touch and the peace that it offered; at first it was electric and warm, and then when he pulled away my selfish body erupted into chaos, demanding more of what I still didn't understand.

Dear God…

The bus came to an abrupt stop a minute later and Nurse Kline jumped to her feet so fast… "Who did it?" She demanded. Her eyes scanned the rows. "You might as well admit to it now and take your punishment like a man *—or woman.* These trips are supposed to be learning experiences, not red carpet opportunities to feed your fucked-up egos! Who did it? Now! I want a name!" I'd never seen Nurse Kline so worked-up. She stormed down the aisle and stopped in front of Thorne—who looked a little turned on and nervous at the same time. Grabbing a fistful of his black shirt, she pulled his muscular body to his feet and hissed, "You're looking awfully nice today, Walsh!"

"It wasn't me!" He snapped back, giving just as much as he was receiving.

She tightened her grip on his shirt and he shoved her away. Pointing a sharp white-tip nail at him she shouted, "Oh you better pray like hell it wasn't! When we reach Baylor I'm getting off of this cheesewagon and marching to the first photographer I see, and if he says Thorne Walsh tipped him off, you will be mine asshole."

"Jesus Kline!" Reyes shouted, gaping at her. Her narrow eyes shot to the row in front of Varla where Reyes sat—back straight, poised as ever. *Brave soul…* "No one called. You're being paranoid, are you sure you aren't having a psychotic break?"

Her lips drew into a thin line and she shook her head

—her eyes wild like an untamed beast. "Do not address me so informally, Park."

Reyes held up his hands, surrendering.

"Someone called and I'm going to find out who, and when I do…" Her voice drifted off, a dark promise of what was to come still hovering in the air when she sat back down.

When we arrived at Baylor five minutes later a pack of photographers was ready and waiting for us at the entrance. The parking lot was bare and from what I could see the inside of the mall was a ghost town.

We parked in a row reserved for handicap customers and when the driver killed the engine fifteen or so photographers raced toward the bus, cameras and microphones poised and at the ready.

"Reyes! Reyes! Can I call you that, or do you prefer Reyes?"

Reyes cracked a smile but didn't respond as the cameras started flashing.

"Last week your victim confirmed that she will be attending USC in the fall. She stated part of the reason for moving west for college was because of you—do you have anything to say about that?"

"Varla—Tina Jeffries from Enquirer Magazine—is it true the upcoming legal drama on Netflix was inspired by you?"

I remained seated as the flashbulbs lit up the inside of the bus, kaleidoscope colors bouncing off the windows. It was like the first day of my trial all over again; everywhere I turned a camera was pointed in my direction, ready to capture every moment.

Some patients were excited to get their extra fifteen minutes of fame and blew kisses at the window—others professed their love for someone back home. "*I know your mom hates me, Beth, but I promise I only have eyes for you! I'll never shove a dildo up her ass again!"*

The doors to the bus splayed open with a creak.

Nurse Kline rose to attention. The cameras continued to go crazy, but inside the bus there was nothing but a tense silence as her sharp finger pointed at everyone. "If any of you embarrass me you'll find your asses in solitary for a *WEEK*." She threatened. Dark eyes filled with pure rage, she shot her finger at the window and muttered, "They might love you and that's fine—but remember you are the property of the state of North Carolina," Her lip curled up "and there is nothing cool about being told when to take a shit."

The word "bitch" was muttered several times as everyone scrambled to form a straight line in the center of the aisle. No one was allowed to step foot off of the bus without an ankle monitor.

"If you are in the safety zone the light on the monitor will stay green." Nurse Kline informed us. "If you try to run it will turn red and every cop within a forty mile radius will be out here hunting for you. Tasers, tear gas—everything will be at their disposal to find you. Do you understand? This is serious. Do not run away."

Miss Maroon stood behind her with a clipboard and a fanny pack wrapped around her waist. "Make sure to see me to get your allowance before you leave."

"And don't spend it on weapons, cords, or rope. Anything that would be considered a safety risk is not allowed on this bus." Nurse Kline warned. "You might want to think about that before slamming your parents hard earned money onto the counter."

Since Laces was in front of me he reached Nurse Kline first, and as I watched her strap the monitor around the ankle of his washed-out jeans my heart really started to pound. The pounding was for two reasons—one, she had abused her power and slept with Laces and was probably getting some sort of high touching his calf—and two, I had never been restrained before with technology and therefore didn't fully trust the method.

Nurse Kline's hand seemed to linger on his body longer than anyone else. *Or maybe it was just me.* The process of watching her hands jerk back and forth on the strap seemed like it took hours. A surge of jealousy I didn't know existed grabbed hold of me as she trailed a bony finger up his leg and toward his thigh. I wanted to reach forward, grab the pointy instrument she was using to turn the monitor's on, and stab her eyes out with it.

Molester…

Laces didn't make anything of the gesture. For all I knew he was used to this type of behavior, and that thought only added to the jealousy burning in my gut. I needed to have a talk with him. *Yes…* this type of behavior was not appropriate. Not now. Not ever.

Miss Maroon passed a black wallet over Nurse Kline's shoulder. "Here you go, Laces." Laces shoved it in his back pocket and turned around to watch Nurse Kline slip the monitor around my ankle. I must've not been as skilled at faking my disdain like everyone else because he asked, "What's wrong?"

"Nothing." I said when Nurse Kline knelt down to turn on my monitor.

He jerked his chin. "What's with the resting bitch face?" He pressed.

My cheeks flushed and I didn't answer. Before I got off of the bus Miss Maroon informed me that my parents hadn't added any money to my allowance—which meant the only thing I would be able to buy was lunch with the meal voucher the mall had given everyone. Her eyes were sympathetic as she handed me the voucher, but my expression didn't change. I expected as much long before I found out about the trip, so I wasn't too disappointed.

The cameras were still going strong when I stepped down the bus. Laces was waiting at the bottom—arm extended, hand ready for mine—with a sexy grin on his gorgeous face. "Your freedom awaits, milady."

SEVENTEEN

Gambrielle

It took twenty minutes to get off of the bus and inside Baylor Mall. The moment my foot connected with the concrete, loud, eager voices filled the air and I was blinded. Photographers stormed forward, pushing and squeezing through to try and get an interview.

Just like court... The thought put a bad taste in my mouth. This was supposed to be a special day to relax my body and regain my strength before heading back to the confines of the asylum, but instead it had turned into a media circus complete with microphones, news vans, sharpies, and the latest magazine covers.

Laces' fingers were intertwined with mine, his free arm protectively shielding me as we navigated through the chaos. He took it in stride—grinning and winking at the cameras as though he were walking the red carpet at the Grammys.

And it wasn't just him.

Varla and Reyes seemed to relish the opportunity; they posed together, his hand on her hip, just like my mother made me do the night of junior prom. Varla would make cute faces at the camera and blow kisses, while Reyes stood beside her, cocky grin in full swing.

Thorne had found a cozy spot off near a tulip flower garden and was knee deep in conversation with a few news reporters. "No, I haven't talked to her family and I don't want to." He was referring to his ex, the one who had cheated and then hung herself in a warehouse. "One of these days her mother is going to have to accept that her daughter was a lying, cheating whore. Not that there's anything wrong with whores—I bag them all the time—but own your shit."

Nurse Kline was standing a few feet away and quickly intervened. "I think that's enough for today." she said, pulling at Thorne's elbow. "He's off of his meds. It's a really trying time for him."

"He appears lucid to me." A reporter noted.

Nurse Kline kicked the back of Thorne's knee with her foot and he tumbled forward, groaning as he fell to the ground. "You call this lucid? Please, the boy can barely stand."

"Why do you do this?"

"I'm not doing anything." Nurse Kline said, helping Thorne to his feet. She patted him on the back once, twice, and said, "There you go, Walsh. Are you feeling okay?"

The reporter smirked. "You can't protect *them* forever. People want to know *their* stories."

"Too bad."

"Other young people are going through the same thing —" before he had a chance to finish his statement, Nurse Kline yanked Laces forward and pushed us through the entrance of Baylor Mall. A few orderlies rounded up the rest of the patients and before we were given the okay to freely roam Nurse Kline took it upon herself to use the moment as a learning opportunity.

"Everything you say will follow you outside of this institution." She warned. "It might seem cool right now to be on the cover of national magazines, but one day the interest will dry up and then what? You think people want to hire a guy that brags about his dead ex-girlfriend to the Enquirer?" Her eyes cut to Thorne. "Think with your brain, not your wallet, asshole."

"Someone is not happy today." I murmured through the corner of my lips.

"Just wait until it's time to leave. With the way she runs around looking for everyone you'd think she was a patient." Laces snickered.

We were released shortly after, but not before being told to be back at the entrance at 4:00 p.m sharp. Those who didn't return at the allotted time would face a special punishment, courtesy of Nurse Kline. I didn't know what she had cooked up, nor did I want to find out.

The mall wasn't as big as the one back in Charlotte, but it had all of the necessities that mattered to most consumers, like a food court and children's playground. Since I wasn't given an allowance I decided to let Laces take the reins and the first stop on his list was, surprisingly, a cell phone store.

"What are we doing?" I asked as he pulled me toward the back. A nice display of the latest touchscreen phones were on top of a glass shelf. Despite the photographers and Nurse Kline's threatening speech, I had been calm for most of the trip. Keyword, calm. Until now, anyway. "We shouldn't be in here!"

We weren't allowed cell phones. It was up there at the top of the list of contraband right next to sharp objects and shoelaces.

"The rules are subjective." Laces said. He picked up the latest iPhone and slid his finger across the screen.

149

A nervous chuckle escaped my lips. "They seemed pretty clear to me." *Put it down, put it down, put it down…*

"Which one do you like?" Laces held out two phones. I wasn't tech savvy and thought they both looked the exact same. Seeing my discomfort, he placed the cell phones back in their holders and cupped my chin. "You need to relax."

"I can't."

Laces grinned and my heart skipped a beat. "If anything comes of it I'll take the blame, stray." He tapped my nose and whispered, "you need to live a little."

I wanted to live, really I did, but I also didn't want to spend 48 hours in solitary confinement—which I could've swore was the punishment for first time cell phone offenders. A sales associate strolled over wearing a nice black shirt and a big smile, and my stomach dipped. "Anything I can help you with?"

I grabbed Laces' arm and started pulling. "No, thank you. I just remembered I don't have any money so…" It was my last attempt at saving us.

Laces jerked his arm away. "Stop that shit. People will think you're trying to kidnap me."

I frowned and slowly released him. "I didn't get an allowance." I admitted, flushing. "And if I did I wouldn't spend it on black market contraband!"

"We're not buying drugs!" Laces scolded me.

The sales associate raised a brow at us. "I am an authorized cell dealer." He assured me.

Before he had the opportunity to say anything else Laces grabbed my elbow and ushered me to the nearest corner like a disobedient child. "I'm going to give you some truth— and for just a minute I want you to block out the good girl part of your brain, soak it in, and—Live. With. Me." Laces instructed in a serious tone.

I swallowed. "But…I can't go to solitary. If I do I won't get a pass to go home and I need my pass!" Without it I wouldn't be able to find Elizabeth's diary and Joe would continue to roam free.

Laces placed both hands on my shoulders and squeezed. "We're not allowed cell phones because they want to monitor who we speak with on the outside. You're not going to be talking to anyone on the outside. Your cell phone will be programmed to call and text one number: MINE. And where will I be?"

Hawthorne…

I opened my mouth to protest and he quickly put his finger to my lips. "No. Stop thinking like a good girl and live in this moment with me."

Okay…just breathe. He was dead set on this, and when Laces was dead set on something there was no changing his mind. Peeking up at him with a doubtful gaze, I bit my lip. I knew what we were about to do was wrong, but one look at his playful eyes and I didn't care. "We'll only be using it to talk to each other?"

Laces' eyes darkened. "Only us." He vowed.

My eyes fell to the cream carpet. I didn't like the idea, but the thought of having something that was just ours outweighed the bad by a ton. Despite my insistence of wanting a cheap cell he did his own thing and picked out the latest iPhone models that had just hit the market. When the sales associate slid mine across the counter and I got a good look at the shiny glass beaming back at me, my stomach did a few somersaults; I hadn't realized how much I had missed the normal things in life until now.

"I'm going to pay you back." I said, beaming up at him. "Whenever I get out of here and get a job, that is."

"Consider it a gift." Laces insisted.

"No."

"YES."

"I am not your charity case. I'll pay you back and that's that." I said, looking away. I knew all too well what it was like to owe someone and the strings that came attached with such a debt. Joe never let me forget it and often tortured me with it every time an unexpected expense came up. It was one of the many tools he used to stay in control.

"I don't know why women make such a big deal about money." Laces said, handing the associate his credit card. "A good boy takes care of his woman."

"You're not a good boy, remember?" I murmured through the corner of my lips.

"Thank fuck for that." Laces said with a roguish grin. He put his credit card back in his wallet, thanked the associate, and steered me out of the cell phone store, grinning. "Bad boys are better, anyways."

"I am *dy-ing* to know your logic with that one…"

"Good boys open doors, bad boys close them."

My face screwed up as we passed a sporty clothing store. "That is the most ridiculous thing I have ever heard."

Laces held up his hand and started ticking his fingers off, "Good boys open doors, bank accounts, and hearts." He cut his eyes to me, "A bad boy will close the door that's been left open, fix the debt you acquired because the good boy, shithead, was off spoiling his mistress, and he will close the hole left in your heart."

"And what if the good boy keeps opening doors? Accounts? Hearts?" Even though my mother had been dealt the worst hand imaginable when it came to men, I still wanted to believe there were some good men out there. I wanted to believe that for every one Joe walking this earth that there were five great men not too far behind him. My heart told me it was a romantic notion, that one had to kiss a few frogs before she found her amazing prince. My brain, however, didn't see eye-to-eye, and kept insisting that type of thinking was naïve.

Laces handed me my new iPhone and flashed his pearly whites. "You want my honest opinion, milady?"

I tucked it into my front skirt pocket and said, "I want Lincoln's honest opinion. Not Laces."

He leaned toward me, his musky scent slamming into my lungs as he whispered, "They are one in the same."

Stopping at the elevator that led to the second floor, I pushed the up button and shook my head. "No, they're not." The elevator dinged and he looked genuinely intrigued as we stepped inside. "Laces is your heart. Lincoln is your soul."

As the elevator lifted his back fell against the glass window and he turned his head. There was a storm brewing in his blue eyes, a fight that couldn't be won just yet. "Some would say I don't have either."

"Those people are idiots." I said, letting out a low smile. "A heartless, bad boy would've left me to fend for myself with Dr. Folton." I shivered at the thought of the pervy old geezer making his own sexual entrances, I leaned toward Laces. "Soulless men don't care about Emily Bronte, either."

His dark eyes cut to me. "You think too highly of me."

"Maybe."

As we got off of the elevator and headed north toward a trendy art store called Up The Wall, I noticed several women taking second glances as we passed by; their eyes traveled up and down his body, lingering on his buff chest and chiseled facial features. Even the grandmothers. No one was immune. He had a presence that demanded attention.

"I think you're going to give that grandma on the bench a stroke." I said once we were inside Up The Wall. Sans the associate, the art supply store was a ghost town. Laces had found his calling in the middle of the store and was in artist mode, studying the vast collection of different sized charcoal pencils. Plucking a few packs from the holder, he held them up like a trophy and thanked the high heavens. In doing so the bottom of his shirt lifted, revealing a toned stomach leading down to that V that had the power to make the smart girls dumb. My eyes widened and my heart picked up.

So did the grandma's. Dropping her yogurt into a trashcan she adjusted her bifocals and smiled—which didn't go unnoticed by Laces. After his dramatic show he grabbed a shopping basket and dropped his pencils inside, winking at the grandma as he moved toward the sketch-pads. "I'm about to make that woman's day." He told me.

"Hmm?"

"The last time she got laid, condoms weren't on the market." Laces said, passing off his basket. Grinning like a possum, he reached for the hem of his shirt and pulled it over his head in that way boys do. Yes, I was certain the grandma was going to have a heart attack.

It was the first time I had seen him shirtless, and he did not disappoint. Not that I wanted him to, *per say*, but part of me had held on to hope that there would be a few flaws so I wouldn't be so self-conscious. A man of his caliber—of his status—was expected to have some wear-and-tear; one didn't just enter an asylum looking like a sculpture of Zeus.

But then again, most men weren't Laces.

Every groove was smooth and taut.

Every muscle defined to perfection by genetics, *or God*…the way the muscles flexed in his upper biceps as he tossed his shirt into the basket, like they had a mind of their own...*Dear Lord...*

Perfect sun-kissed tan.

Perfect physique.

And the V-crease, oh the aforementioned crease, had returned from it's two-minute sabbatical, ready to take over the world with him. As a precaution, my hand flew to my jaw to check that it was still closed. *No.* Crap. I gestured toward his godly physique—and squeaked. Yes, I actually squeaked.

"Come!" He called out. His unnatural ass shifted against the fabric of his tight jeans as he stomped toward the back of the store in all of his shirtless glory.

"You have to wear a shirt, sir!" The cashier called out to him as he snatched a couple of erasers. "Sir!"

Laces swirled around on his heel to face him, and flashed the biggest grin. "I'm classified legally insane by the beautiful state of North Carolina." He took a step forward and toyed with the sleeve of the black and red flannel shirt tied around his jeans. "I don't have to wear shit if I don't want to. Now stop giving me a hard time and start ringing shit up."

EIGHTEEN

Gambrielle

"I CANNOT DO THIS."

No. My mother, who had already disowned me, would start pulling in other family members to disown me as well. No one in our family had ever gotten a tattoo. Not if they wanted to stay *in* the family. Hugging the art supplies that Laces had purchased from Up The Wall, I shook my head for what felt like the twentieth time that day as Laces pointed at a beautiful, white butterfly in the tattoo portfolio he had been looking through. "You need ink. TODAY."

Nope.

"I'm thinking a sexy butterfly with some skulls above that nice ass of yours." Laces face split into a wide grin. "I could draw it for you, if you want? Give it a more *personal* touch…"

I held up my finger, "Or…you can get a tattoo on your pelvic," I pointed an unsteady finger at the general direction of his crotch and felt nothing but flames burning up my cheeks. "That would give me something to look at while you're sketching a dagger through Bey's chest." I liked my idea. I liked it very much.

Mmhmm.

No pain for me *and* I would reap the rewards.

Laces smiled, thinking about it. "I fail to see where I benefit from this."

My chest rumbled. "It's the gift that keeps on giving." Every time he took off his shirt, I would be rewarded with the gift of his glorious, lean, tattooed body. What more could a girl ask for? *Not a damn thing.*

A bubbly tattoo artist named Mark, who had a blinding, yellow mullet, plucked his toothpick out of his mouth and leaned across the black, marble counter. "I'm going to help you out here, brother. If you want to get laid this century, you'll go into that back room and drop your drawers." He said in an uppity tone.

Staring down at me, Laces' eyebrows raised inquiringly. "It that what this is? A hostage negotiation?"

My smile turned into a chuckle. "Maybe."

His compelling, magnetic blue eyes never left mine as he said in a low, husky voice "Guess we better book that tattoo, Mark."

Everything inside me melted. *He's actually going through with it!* I couldn't believe it.

Maybe we could make this work, I thought as Laces winked at me and signed proceeded to sign the consent papers for Mark. Whatever we were was not conventional by any means. Far from it. But what was? *Right?*

And then it happened.

Fate, decided to step in.

"There he is!" Hearing what sounded like Nurse Kline's voice in the near distance, I glanced over my shoulder. Almost immediately my body went numb when I finally saw who was following behind her.

Joe.

My stepfather!

"Oh my God." I whispered, grabbing my chest. I felt like I was about to have a heart attack!

"There you are!" Joe proclaimed. "We've been looking everywhere for you!"

I'll bet you have...

Laces quickly scribbled his signature and like me, looked in the direction of the noise. "Oh shit!" He hissed.

Joe had the biggest smile plastered across his heartless face. "Lincoln! We've been looking everywhere for you, son!"

My heart stopped as the bastard pushed past me and threw his arms over Laces back.

"Dad, what are you doing here?" Laces' voice was kind, but I sensed a hint of annoyance behind it.

Could've made it work.

To Be Continued...

Ready for book 2?
If so, preorder Lincoln* now, then add to your Goodreads TBR!
*Release Date, cover, and blurb coming soon!

About Tempi

Tempi Lark is a USA Today Bestselling author of New Adult and YA Romance. She lives in Tennessee with her husband, son, and enormous book collection. She enjoys binge-watching Netflix, dancing in her pajamas, and writing about crazy alphas that can't seem to get it together.

Acknowledgments

I want to thank my husband for putting up with me writing in a room for 5 hours at a time. Throughout my career he has always been my "constant". Whenever I have needed advice or any type of support he was always ready. There were many times I wanted to give up and he kept me aligned to finish. I love you, madly. XOXO. Also, thank you to my son for being an inspiration like no other. He has endured many struggles over the years and kept smiling, kept going.

J.E. PARKER. You reached out to me when I was in a really dark place in my life. We forged a close bond and you took me under your wing with no questions asked. For two years I watched your career develop and you kindly offered any/all insight. Because of your wisdom I found my footing early-on and was given a head start that other's could only dream of. *You write it and we'll market it.* I couldn't ask for better best friend. (P.S. That mafia book of yours is gonna to be lit! lol)

Special thanks to my editor, Sara Miller, for pulling this one out of both of our asses. You understand my vision and never try to change my voice. *hugs* Instead of trying to tone down my "southern twang" you find ways to build on it. Thank you, lady!

MY FABULOUS VETERANS. Skyla, Katie, Elizabeth, Judith, Alondra, Tanja, & Mahshad. 10 YEARS LATER & here we are. *grins* Thank you so much for believing in me and sticking around for the last 10 years. Laces was not the journey we started with, but everything this book became I contribute to the early days. You guys gave me my start and made me really fall in love with writing. I remember posting to the private Facebook profile (the note section) almost everyday for 2 years. There was no money involved; only a dream of one day seeing a group of paranormal men (who kicked some serious ass) displayed on my bookshelf at home. I am forever grateful for your loyalty and look forward to introducing the world to the characters y'all fell in love with so long ago. #Tucksters #Warlords

Thank you to my PA & friend, Maria, for stepping in and taking charge when I wanted to throw in the towel. (Light more candles before the next book!) Thank you for respecting and admiring my work, and for pushing me. You were the driving force behind Laces during the early writing stages and made sure I stuck with it. You believed in this book when no one else did.

Special thanks to Crystal Nelson & Bri Danielle, who beta read early on.

And thanks to Michelle Vasquez, Kenia Fields, and

Mahida Gulzar for your undying support. A huge thank you to my STEET TEAM for kicking ass over the last few months. You guys are the absolute best and I can't wait to jump into the next adventure!
Special shoutout to Greylin Reuss. Thank you for all that you have done.

And lastly, thank you to the readers.
Stay safe, my beautiful creatures.
-T

Made in the USA
Monee, IL
24 November 2021

82809830R00098